INFINITE LEGACY

The 7 Principles of Creating
a Lasting Impact With Your Life

By
**Ivan Misner, Ph.D.
Greg Davies
Julian Lewis**

Copyright© 2024 Ivan R. Misner, Greg Davies, and Julian Lewis

All Rights Reserved

Authors: Ivan Misner, PhD, Greg Davies, Julian Lewis

Editor: Heidi Scott Giusto, PhD

Cover Design: Olivia Pro Design

Layout Design: Lyubomyr Yatsk

Givers Gain® and BNI® are registered trademarks of BNI and are used with permission.

For more information on other books, visit: www.IvanMisner.com

SECTION ONE

CHAPTER 1
YOUR LEGACY IS YOUR CHOICE

Sitting at a table in a cafe in the middle of nineteenth-century Paris, a successful inventor, industrialist, and millionaire drank freshly roasted coffee and set about updating himself on the news and current affairs of the day.

While we benefit from notifications on our phones, streaming news 24 hours a day and the ability to name search any of our contemporaries, for this gentleman the best way to keep up with the achievements of his peer group and to judge his own, was to read the obituary section in his daily newspaper.

He turned the pages, scanning names, ages, and accolades, when suddenly he stopped; his eyes froze, locked and fixated on his very own name.

Once the initial shock of seeing himself in the obituary section subsided and concluding that it was mistake due sloppy journalism (in fact, it was a case of mistaken identity with his brother Ludvig who had died of heart failure), his curiosity impelled him to read on.

can genuinely make a difference in the world. By discovering and embracing our unique talent, we change the world and ensure that our legacy endures.

In this book, we will show you how you can deliver for your family, your community, your country, or the whole world, a lasting legacy that will inspire others and become infinite.

Some legacies are, by their very nature, infinite.

Take, for example, a family tradition that began simply as a good idea and has been passed down through generations, growing richer and more meaningful with each iteration. Many families have such a tradition in their history.

Similarly, the substantial philanthropic contributions of someone like Andrew Carnegie, who donated an astounding $350 million between 1881 and 1919, which continues to impact society profoundly. His endowments have supported libraries, education, and scientific research, proving that a well-considered legacy can resonate indefinitely.

These legacies have stood the test of time and shaped countless lives. Their influence has no foreseeable end, as they perpetuate values, knowledge, and opportunities across ages and geographies.

Such enduring legacies remind us of how thoughtful actions have lasting impact, which inspires us to contribute our own enduring gifts to the world.

Most legacies do not begin with the expectation of becoming infinite. Instead, they start as small, inspired actions that gradually evolve into something more significant and enduring. To create an Infinite Legacy, one must first take the initial step of seeking to make a positive impact. Drawing inspiration from this book's insights and stories, readers are encouraged to explore ways to contribute meaningfully to the world around them. This could be through acts of kindness, innovations, or community service.

> **Most legacies do not begin with the expectation of becoming infinite. Instead, they start as small, inspired actions that gradually evolve into something more significant and enduring.**

Once these efforts begin to shape positive change, you can consider formalizing them into a more structured legacy project. Such projects might include establishing a charitable fund to support ongoing causes, writing a book to share knowledge and inspire future generations, or creating a prize to reward and encourage specific achievements. Each of these endeavors extends the reach of one's impact, ensuring that it continues to resonate and inspire long after the initial act. By thoughtfully planning and dedicating resources to these legacy projects, individuals can create lasting legacies.

We strongly recommend maintaining the authenticity of your legacy, a concept central to this book and deeply rooted in existentialist philosophy. In existentialism, authenticity is defined as the extent to which an individual's actions align with their beliefs and desires despite external pressures to conform. Embracing authenticity offers profound benefits when it comes to legacy building.

First, when our actions are in harmony with our genuine interests and values, we are more likely to sustain a deep, enduring passion for our endeavors. This passion is crucial, as it fuels our commitment and resilience, enabling us to nurture and grow our legacy over time. A legacy built on such authentic foundations is more likely to evolve into an Infinite Legacy—one that continues to influence and inspire beyond our immediate presence.

Second, living authentically ensures that our unique perspective is preserved and shared within the broader tapestry of human experience. By staying true to ourselves and our best values, we contribute a distinct voice to the virtual legacy library—a metaphorical collection of human achievements and philosophies. This enriches the diversity of legacies available for future generations to learn from and ensures that our personal view of the world is represented and remembered.

Maintaining this authenticity requires continuous reflection and a willingness to act according to our true selves, even when challenging. By doing so, we lead more fulfilling lives and lay the groundwork for legacies that truly reflect who we are and what we stand for.

Our primary goal with this book is to underscore and magnify the power of legacy as a profound gift to the world, one that has the potential to make it a markedly better place for all. We aim to inspire a wide audience to engage in acts of goodness and to contemplate the enduring impact of their own legacies. As more individuals strive to leave a positive mark, a ripple effect occurs, encouraging and enabling others to contribute their own legacies. This cumulative effect creates a virtuous cycle, where each successive contribution builds upon the last, enhancing our collective ability to create positive change.

> **Our primary goal with this book is to underscore and magnify the power of legacy as a profound gift to the world, one that has the potential to make it a markedly better place for all.**

By fostering this mindset, we not only improve our immediate environments but also set in motion a series of actions that elevate global communities. This upward spiral of goodwill and positive legacy acts as a catalyst for an ever-improving world—a world where each person's contribution is valued and where each of us has the opportunity to thrive. In the following pages, we explore various ways individuals can make such contributions, from small, everyday acts to grand, life-long projects. We delve into the stories of those who have already made significant impacts, drawing lessons and insights that can guide others in crafting their legacies.

We aim to create a narrative that not only celebrates the achievements of remarkable legacy-builders but also serves as a call to action for every reader to consider how they too can contribute to a better, more sustainable world. By championing the power of legacy, we hope to encourage a future where everyone is empowered to leave a positive, lasting impact.

> **By championing the power of legacy, we hope to encourage a future where everyone is empowered to leave a positive, lasting impact.**

After reading this book, you will gain a deeper appreciation for the importance of legacy and its relevance to your personal life. This understanding will extend beyond mere theory, as you will discover numerous innovative ideas tailored to help you determine what your unique and authentic legacy might entail. Each page is designed to inspire and equip you with the knowledge necessary to identify and embrace your own distinctive contributions to the world.

Furthermore, this book will guide you through a structured process to begin crafting your own Infinite Legacy. We provide practical advice, strategic planning tools, and inspirational examples spanning various fields and interests, enabling you to align your legacy initiatives with your deepest values and aspirations. By the conclusion of this book, you won't just be planning to leave a legacy; you'll be on the path to creating a lasting impact that resonates with your personal vision and goals.

Whether you're looking to influence your community, innovate in your professional field, or impart lasting values to future generations, this book will serve as your roadmap. It aims not only to inform but also to transform your perspective, motivating you to take action and begin the meaningful journey toward leaving a profound and enduring mark on the world.

The notion of legacy, often entwined with ideas of wealth or historical impact, is deeply philosophical. We would like to paraphrase Jean-Paul Sartre, a towering figure in existentialist philosophy, who provides a compelling perspective on legacy through his poignant observation in his play No Exit: "One always dies too soon or too late and yet their life is complete at that moment, with a line drawn neatly under it ready for the summing up." You are your deeds in life and little more. This thought opens a unique avenue to explore the concept of legacy as a record of achievements and a testament to our actions and their alignment with our existential beliefs.

> **"One always dies too soon or too late and yet their life is complete at that moment, with a line drawn neatly under it ready for the summing up." You are your deeds in life and little more.**

Sartre's existentialism puts forward that existence precedes essence, meaning that humans first exist without any predetermined essence and then, through their actions, create their essence. Therefore, the legacy we leave behind is essentially the essence we've sculpted through our choices and actions throughout our lives. When Sartre says one's life is "complete" at the moment of death, he suggests that whatever one has done up to that point constitutes one's entire essence, one's legacy. This finality is not about the timing of death but about the wholeness and completeness of life as reflected through our deeds.

In practical terms, Sartre's philosophy urges us to consider how each decision and action contributes to the legacy we are building. Whether it's a career-long endeavor, interpersonal relationships, or even fleeting interactions, our actions accumulate to form a coherent narrative about who we are. For example, consider someone like Mother Teresa, whose life of service and compassion left a legacy of profound charity and humanitarian work. In contrast, an entrepreneur like Steve Jobs left a legacy of innovation and high standards, fundamentally shaping technological progress and corporate culture. Both figures embody Sartre's idea that we are our deeds, and little more, but those deeds can resonate on a vast, sometimes global scale.

However, one does not need to be famous to leave a significant legacy. Every individual can impact others and contribute to the collective human experience. Take, for instance, a teacher whose dedication shapes the minds and attitudes of countless students or a volunteer who spends their weekends feeding the homeless. These actions might not garner global recognition, but they create profound ripples across society, much like a stone thrown into a calm lake creates a wide-spread ripple effect. This democratization of legacy, as proposed by Sartre, emphasizes that the sum of one's life, the neat line under it, is drawn through everyday acts of authenticity and choice.

> **A teacher whose dedication shapes the minds and attitudes of countless students or a volunteer who spends their weekends feeding the homeless. These actions might not garner global recognition, but they create profound ripples across society.**

In the contemporary context, the challenge to legacy-building is the distraction and divergence presented by modern life. Social media and the digital age, emphasizing transient, often superficial snapshots of existence, can dilute the perception of a coherent, action-based legacy. Sartre's philosophy invites a return to authenticity, urging individuals to act in ways that are true to their beliefs and desires rather than conforming to external expectations.

investments, and other assets that are passed down from one generation to another. These assets can provide financial security for future generations, and they can be used to fund education, start businesses, or support charitable causes. However, financial legacies can also come with a great deal of responsibility, as they must be managed and invested wisely to ensure that they continue to provide benefits for future generations.

Another very important aspect of legacy is the impact that we have on the world around us. This can include the way that we treat others, the causes that we support, and the way that we live our lives. These are the things that will be remembered long after we are gone, and they will shape the way that future generations see us. It is important to consider the impact that we want to have on the world and to strive to make a positive difference in the lives of others.

Legacies can also take the form of knowledge and skills. These are things that we pass down to future generations through education and mentorship. They can include anything from technical skills and knowledge of a particular field to more general life skills such as critical thinking, problem-solving, and emotional intelligence. This type of legacy can be incredibly valuable as it equips future generations with the tools needed to navigate the world and to make a positive impact in their own way.

Our cultural heritage is also a form of legacy. It is the sum of the traditions, customs, beliefs, and values that we pass down from one generation to another. It encompasses things like language, religion, and art, and it plays a crucial role in shaping our identity and sense of belonging. Cultural legacies can be incredibly powerful as they connect us to our past and help us to understand who we are and where we come from.

Last, one of the most powerful legacies we can leave is the example of our own lives. The way we live our lives, the choices we make, and the values we uphold, will all be remembered long after we are gone. Our example can inspire future generations and can shape the way that they see the world. It is important to strive to live a life that we can be proud of and that will be remembered fondly by those who come after us.

A legacy is a multifaceted concept, and it is important to consider what kind of legacy we want to leave and ensure it aligns with your core purpose and values. In this book, we refer to "Your Why," which is in modern times widely linked to Simon Sinek's theory from his book *Start with Why*. "Your Why" is a compelling framework that emphasizes the importance of understanding and articulating the core purpose that drives individuals and organizations.

Rooted in the idea that true motivation and long-lasting success stems from a deep sense of purpose, Sinek argues that identifying "Your Why"—the fundamental reason behind your actions—can inspire and guide you toward meaningful achievements. By focusing on this intrinsic motivation, rather than only the "what" or "how," Sinek believes individuals and organizations can build a more authentic and impactful legacy, fostering trust and loyalty among their followers and making a lasting difference in the world.

When we identify our why and align our legacy with that why, the world around us in some small way becomes brighter. This stirs in us a motivation to make things better for others. Even the simplest of actions, such as planting a tree, is life-giving and legacy-creating. As we end this chapter, we invite you to reflect on the following Greek proverb: A society grows great when old men plant trees in whose shade they shall never sit.

A society grows great when old men plant trees in whose shade they shall never sit.

CHAPTER 4
IMPACT VS. LEGACY

While this book is about leaving a gift to the world, there are times when it is more important to make an immediate impact and not leave a legacy.

If we were caught in the blazing sun at high noon and we came across a fallen tree, planting the seeds and waiting for them to grow would not offer us the shade needed in the same way that fashioning a shelter from the branches and leaves would.

We may see a situation that requires massive and immediate action to solve a current problem, rather than establishing ongoing support, which will eventually lead to change for the benefit of all.

This was certainly the case with Live Aid.

In 1984, Michael Buerk, a BBC newsreader delivered an emotional and hard-hitting report containing images of starving children in Ethiopia. The BBC news crews were the first to document the famine, describing it in biblical proportions.

Claire Bertschinger, a young and compassionate nurse, found herself at the heart of an overwhelming humanitarian crisis in Ethiopia, surrounded by 85,000 starving and desperate people. The task she was entrusted with was one that no one should ever have to bear: deciding which children would be granted access to the scarce food supplies at the feeding station, and which would be left behind, too weak to be saved. This unbearable responsibility weighed heavily on her, leading to a profound sense of guilt and trauma.

The act of physically marking the children who were chosen to be fed haunted Bertschinger for years. The emotional burden was so immense that it took her until 2005 to begin openly discussing her experience. During an interview with BBC News when reflecting on her role, she poignantly stated, "I felt like a Nazi sending people to the death camps. Why was I in this situation? Why was it possible in a time of such abundance that some had food and others did not? It's not right."

The broadcast of this harrowing report reached far and wide, striking a chord with viewers across the globe. One such viewer was Bob Geldof, the renowned pop star, who was deeply moved by what he saw. Reflecting on Bertschinger's unimaginable burden, Geldof remarked, "In her was vested the power of life and death. She had become God-like, and that is unbearable for anyone."

The impact of the report was immediate and far-reaching. The British public, moved by the plight of those suffering in Ethiopia, responded with an outpouring of donations to various charities. The BBC's global reach ensured that the crisis received widespread attention, prompting international concern. Remarkably, Burke's report was broadcast in its entirety on a major United States news channel, an unprecedented event at the time, further amplifying the call for action and bringing the world's attention to the devastating famine in Ethiopia.

This moment in history not only highlighted the profound personal struggles of those like Bertschinger, who were on the frontlines of humanitarian aid, but it also demonstrated the power of media to mobilize global action in the face of overwhelming tragedy.

Geldof picked up the phone to the lead singer of Ultravox, Midge Ure. They had previously worked together on a charity benefit show called The Secret Policeman's Ball. Ure had also seen the report, and they agreed they needed to act.

They quickly co-wrote the song 'Do They Know It's Christmas?' and contacted colleagues in the music industry to persuade them to record the single under the title Band Aid. They also wanted their fellow musicians' technicians and producers to do this for free.

The song was recorded at the Sarm West Studios in Notting Hill on November 25, 1984, and was released four days later. The now famous video shows megastars of the time, smiling, laughing, and in Phil Collins' case, wearing a particularly ugly cardigan.

The song topped the charts for five weeks and became that year's Christmas Number One single. It became the fastest selling track ever in Britain and raised £8 million rather than the £70,000 that Geldof and Ure had initially targeted. Because of the success of the single, Geldof then set his sights on a larger target, a huge concert to raise further funds.

The idea for the Live Aid concert originally came from the lead singer of Culture Club, Boy George. Following a national tour, he had invited some of the participants from the single to join him on stage at Wembley Arena. So overcome by the occasion and seeing a way of perpetuating the goodwill toward the victims of the famine, George suggested a dedicated live event.

On Saturday, July 13, 1985, in multiple venues across the globe, Live Aid began. Seventy-two thousand people in Northwest London flooded into Wembley Arena at the very same time as 89,500 fellow music lovers joined them on the other side of the globe in the John F. Kennedy Stadium in Philadelphia. In addition to these two central hub concerts, and inspired by the initiative, further events were held in the Soviet Union, Canada, Japan, Yugoslavia, Austria, Australia, and West Germany.

One of the largest satellite linkups of all time led to a television broadcast, with an estimated audience of 1.9 billion people across 150 nations, which represented nearly 40 percent of the world population at the time.

The impact of this collective action was obvious. More than £150 million (£350 million adjusted for inflation, 2022) was raised as a direct result of the concerts. The publicity generated encouraged Western nations to make enough surplus grain available to end the immediate hunger crisis in Africa. It was an immediate impact that was needed to help the hundreds of thousands of starving people in Africa; it was not a lasting legacy.

If we were to see a person dying of thirst, a glass of water would have a massive and immediate impact on their quality of life. If you can impact the situation at hand, to benefit those in need, this is always the right thing to do.

If you can impact the situation at hand, to benefit those in need, this is always the right thing to do.

In addition to these amazing acts of impact, we believe that following the 7 Principles of Infinite Legacy will enable everyone to help those currently in need with acts of impact AND create a lasting and perpetuating gift to the world around them.

CHAPTER 5
THE 7 PRINCIPLES OF INFINITE LEGACY

We have found that it is easier to wrap your head around concepts when they are laid out as identifiable principles that one can follow. With that in mind, we would like to introduce you to the 7 Principles of Infinite Legacy, which if followed, will ensure that your gift to the world, whatever you decide it will be, will continue once your time on earth has ceased.

We will outline them here in this chapter and will then cover them in more detail in the following chapters.

1. **<u>Be proud of the legacy you leave.</u>**

    Everyone leaves a legacy, so be aware of that and create one that allows you to be proud of yours. Legacy is a conscious choice. Make it an Intentional Legacy and not an Accidental Legacy.

    We all have the opportunity to build a legacy to be proud of. We can even change the direction of our current legacy to fall within the framework of our morals and values. Imagine your great-great-grandchild telling the story of your life and legacy to your great-great-great-great-grandchild. What would fill you with pride?

Imagine your great-great-grandchild telling the story of your life and legacy to your great-great-great-great-grandchild. What would fill you with pride?

---

2. <u>**Give what you can afford when you can afford it.**</u>

   Give from your saucer, not from your cup.

   When building an Infinite Legacy, we must respect the resources we have when we go to use them. Sometimes we may only have the ability to apply our time. This may then evolve into using our talents, and, last, we may be able to donate our treasure.

   Each of the above is a diminishing resource when we go to use it. We have to practice discernment, so not to deplete our day-to-day resources while still using all we can to build our legacy.

3. <u>**Be guided by your passion.**</u>

   Understand your "why" and align your legacy to it.

   An Infinite Legacy may take years or even decades to establish. It will require effort, dedication, and commitment to reach a stage where it perpetuates and takes on a life of its own. In the early stages of establishing your legacy, you will find it easier to undertake the necessary steps if your subject matter has a base in your own passions. Having a strong "why" that underpins your activities will allow you to overcome any early setbacks or adversity.

4. **Connect with your community.**

    It's not who's in your story—it's whose story are you in? We all have people that have changed our lives in some way. However, the true measure of a meaningful legacy is "whose story are you in?" Whose life have you changed in some positive way?

The true measure of a meaningful legacy is "whose story are you in?" Whose life have you changed in some positive way?

It will be simpler in the short term to start locally and grow globally. In a personal interview with Sir Richard Branson, he suggested that we begin by drawing circles out from where we currently are and see who we can impact within our reach. Start with our family and work out from there to make a bigger impact to our community and beyond. By focusing on our community, we will also find people willing to join us on our journey because we already have commonality with them. Once we have "filled in" our initial circle, we will then be able to draw larger and larger circles, impacting vastly more people and communities as our legacies begin to grow beyond our reach.

Think like Richard.

5. **Act with urgency.**

   Act like someone is watching.

   None of us really know when our time is up. Even great writers like Charles Dickens, William Shakespeare, Geoffrey Chaucer, and Mark Twain had unfinished manuscripts on their desk. We will be judged on the legacies we leave not the ones that we intended.

   Act now, act with urgency, and live without regret.

6. **Think like a stonemason.**

   All stonemasons know they must first build a foundation before the building takes shape. Your legacy may not truly be completed during your lifetime, but the foundations you lay will be used to build something incredible that will benefit the world you leave behind.

Your legacy may not truly be completed during your lifetime, but the foundations you lay will be used to build something incredible that will benefit the world you leave behind.

   Never lose sight of this.

7. **Have an infinite mindset.**

   Create an Infinite Legacy that continues without you involved. The ultimate Infinite Legacy is one that continues to operate and perpetuate without the input of its founder.

> We must always be looking for ways to future-proof our legacy to ensure its impact is eternal.

By recognizing and respecting the 7 Principles of Infinite Legacy, we can ensure that whatever we choose to gift to our family, friends, local community, or beyond, will have the best possible chance to become infinite.

The above principles represent the conceptual aspects of building an Infinite Legacy. In the section and chapters that follow we give you the tactics of how to implement them.

SECTION TWO

CHAPTER 6
HOW DO YOU CHOOSE?

The range of personal and organizational legacy is vast. It can also feel like the opportunity to leave a legacy is out of reach or simply not a priority for you. While it may not be a priority, it is most definitely not "out of reach." All of the authors have had parents, friends, teachers, or mentors who have influenced us in some positive way that has allowed us to pass on that learning to others. It is the powerful ripple effect that legacy can have. No money exchanged hands, no transaction took place, no charitable foundation was created. It was just the simple act of supporting someone in some positive way that left a positive legacy behind from someone we knew.

> **All of the authors have had parents, friends, teachers, or mentors who have influenced us in some positive way that has allowed us to pass on that learning to others. It is the powerful ripple effect that legacy can have.**

All change starts with understanding. People—you—can begin with this understanding and then take the action required to deliver your legacy. Legacy is a lifetime project, and your life is part of your legacy. If we do not act with urgency when crafting our legacy, it might be too late to have the effect we desire.

It is never too early to consider our goals and add legacy-building activities to our blend of undertakings. By respecting the 7 Principles when doing so, we ensure our choice for our legacy project has the very best opportunity to benefit as many people, for as many years, as possible.

When it comes to choosing our cause, we can start immediately regardless of age, as soon as an opportunity comes into view. Later, we provide examples of very young people who started to create a legacy project and have had huge success. There is no need for an ID check when beginning. Start as soon as you can.

There is a perception, one that we are looking to change, that we only start to consider our legacy as we get toward the end of our lives. It is often called something different: end-of-life planning.

However, when end-of-life planning starts is a personal decision. We believe it should be part of our regular thinking all through our adult lives. That way we have the time to put a plan in place and execute it effectively. As we go through life, what happens to us and how we react to it creates the life we lead. It should also be informing our choice of legacy projects. Such an intentional approach allows us to build our legacy even from very humble beginnings into potentially an Infinite Legacy as our mark on the world.

Often our legacy projects will grow from a passion that we create or adopt as part of our working or personal life. There will be many things that look like they could become our legacy. These will come and go as we ourselves grow. If you regularly engage with the idea that you will leave at least one legacy to your family, your community, your country, or the world, then the right legacy will find you as you live your life on purpose.

Living life on purpose means planning and making active decisions about how we spend our time. The opposite is letting life happen to us with no real consideration for the future beyond the next weekend or the next holiday. When we live life intentionally, we can choose to consider our legacy. As we tell the story of many legacies from all angles and all walks of life, let your imagination wander. As you read, allow yourself to be inspired to explore the legacy you want to leave—one day it will hit you clean in the face.

> **Living life on purpose means planning and making active decisions about how we spend our time.**

"I have to do this."

When that happens, you will have found a legacy project. In some ways, we don't choose the legacy; the legacy chooses us. Our responsibility to that project once chosen is to take regular action to make it happen.

> **In some ways, we don't choose the legacy; the legacy chooses us.**

We love the phrase, "when all is said and done, more is said than done." We urge you to be the one who does what they say they are going to do and build your positive legacy.

The following chapters detail examples of the different types of legacy that you could leave. Some may resonate with you, others may wash over you, and that's OK. We hope to help you decide, or at the very least, begin to formulate what your legacy will become—and how to make your legacy infinite.

CHAPTER 7
PRINCIPLE 1: BE PROUD OF THE LEGACY YOU LEAVE – SECRET LEGACY

We hear of many people whose focus for a large proportion of their life is to accumulate wealth and status, only to, one day, be faced with their own mortality. They suddenly realize it will all come to an end. Their renewed focus becomes a drive to leave a mark on the world.

Examples of this include Henry Tate, the sugar magnate of Tate and Lyle fame, who chose the arts to perpetuate his legacy and has four museums named after him: Tate Britain, Tate Modern, Tate Liverpool, and Tate Saint Ives. Andrew Carnegie, in addition to the world-famous Carnegie Hall, had more than 1,600 libraries built in America that bore his name.

In fact, by the end of his life, Andrew Carnegie had given away over 90 percent of his fortune. A story has often been about Carnegie's response to a journalist. When asked about donating such a vast fortune, he responded, "You should see the 10 percent I've got left!" That 10 percent represented $30 million in 1903, which in today's money would be worth approximately $1 billion when adjusted for inflation (not invested).

People often focus on the remaining wealth as a way of diminishing the tremendous impact these industrious juggernauts have had by suggesting that they were never inconvenienced—that they never "suffered" for their acts of giving. We miss the point when we judge such a huge legacy so harshly.

These philanthropists were under no pressure to donate their personal fortunes, and, due to their generosity, hundreds of thousands of lives have been improved. (Consider how many people have benefitted from the libraries Carnegie funded!) Could they have given more? Probably. Could they have given less? Definitely.

Whatever the motivation for this kind of legacy, whether it be some form of represented immortality or a genuine desire to improve the world around them, it is almost impossible to walk into any major city in the established world and not be faced with a building, theater, university, library, or museum from an industrialist from decades or centuries before.

The major issue with this kind of legacy is that time and ideals move on. At some point, how you made your fortune could be, and sometimes should be, scrutinized.

This happened in an extremely public and high-profile way when the bronze statue of an individual from the 1700's was defaced with red paint and removed forcibly from its plinth in the center of Bristol, England during a Black Lives Matter protest and thrown into the harbor. The statue had been erected posthumously in 1895 to reflect the large amount of good that a £71,000 charitable donation had done following the man's death in 1721. However, as early as 1990, controversy swirled around the statue because much of his personal fortune was derived from the slave trade.

The statue was recovered and reinstalled, but then removed. After a brief exhibition, with the red paint still intact, the statue has been stored out of public view ever since. Beware of your behaviors in life; they can come back to haunt you as with this compelling example.

Of course, not everyone who leaves a public legacy will have the source of their fortunes questioned or criticized in the future. But we do not know which practices that are commonplace today will become abhorrent to future generations. Moreover, people frequently question the motives of public displays of generosity.

A different approach is leaving a "Secret Legacy," which allows true acts of giving, kindness, and legacy formation, without any judgement or accusation that it was done for any personal gain or promotion. Numerous high-profile individuals have wanted to see their legacy in action without any form of celebrity or media intrusion. (And many more probably exist who we don't know about because they have successfully kept their secret.)

In today's society, it seems like no charitable donation goes unfilmed. We are bombarded on social media by people buying meals, paying for haircuts, and providing clothing, all while being filmed and shared for likes and views. This reminds us of a point we made in our first book, *Infinite Giving*: "A gift is not a gift if we expect something in return."

In stark contrast to public displays of generosity filmed and shared on social media, the secret legacy has become one of the purest forms of philanthropy.

Wonderful stories abound about Keanu Reeves, Taylor Swift, and Prince—all who have consistently donated anonymously to individuals and organizations with no desire for recognition or attention. We only know of their acts of generosity because the people who benefitted told the world. Even the King himself, Elvis Presley, used to give away Cadillacs to those around him, including one for the Cadillac salesman, with his gifts only coming to light after Presley's passing.

> **In stark contrast to public displays of generosity filmed and shared on social media, the secret legacy has become one of the purest forms of philanthropy.**

One of the biggest embracers of this secret legacy was singer George Michael.

Despite appearing on charitable singles and public appeals throughout his life, Michael insisted on keeping most of his charitable acts out of the eye of the media. These included everything from large cash donations to small acts of kindness that fans shared following his death on December 25, 2016.

Speaking on September 18, 1999, to the *Daily Express*, a United Kingdom newspaper, Michael addressed rumors in a rare recognition of his philanthropy: "To be honest with you, I really don't like to talk about the amount I've given to charity over the years. I know it's very substantial. I don't exactly know what it is, and I don't really like to linger on it."

Upon Michael's death, the social media platform X (formerly Twitter) was flooded with examples of his kindness. Those who shared obviously felt that they had respected his wishes of anonymity and now wanted to tell the world what a wonderful man it had lost.

The magazine *Nursing Standards* shared how following the death of Michael's mother, he threw a free concert exclusively for nurses to say thank you for all they did.

Richard Osman, a United Kingdom quiz show host and television presenter, revealed for the first time that it was Michael who had secretly donated £15,000 to a contestant on Deal or No Deal who failed to win the amount she needed for her IVF treatment.

And radio DJ Mick Brown shared how every Easter during the Help a London Child campaign Michael called-in at exactly 3:30 pm with a £100,000 donation.

There are so many other examples we could explore—from sending an underprivileged child to Lapland, to bidding £55,000 on a guitar at a charitable auction only to hand it back to be auctioned again and working undercover in a homeless soup kitchen—that begin to illustrate the remarkable acts of kindness that George Michael bestowed during his life.

These are, of course, only the ones that we know about; countless others have most likely gone undiscovered or where the recipients are unaware or maintain the donor's anonymity.

The secret legacy does not come with your name on the side of the building. It does, however, allow you to see the good that your gift achieves while you are around to see it.

The secret legacy does not come with your name on the side of the building.

We are strong believers that if you do the right things, for the right reasons, the world catches up. In other words, if you're doing the right things, for the right reasons, you will have a positive impact, whether people notice or not.

What can you do today, with no expectation of recognition or reward, no chance of likes or views, and no desire for peer or public approval, will allow you to experience the joy of creating a secret legacy.

CHAPTER 8
PRINCIPLE 1: BE PROUD OF THE LEGACY YOU LEAVE – YOUR LIVING LEGACY

Dolly Parton, for many the Queen of Country Music, is known for her iconic voice, dazzling rhinestone outfits, and legendary songwriting. However, her legacy extends far beyond the stage and recording studio. Her philanthropic activities have created a living legacy that touches the lives of millions, embodying her deep-rooted values of generosity, empathy, and love for her community. This story delves into the heartwarming journey of Dolly Parton's philanthropy, illustrating how her kindness and vision have made an indelible mark on the world.

Dolly Rebecca Parton was born on January 19, 1946, in a one-room cabin in Locust Ridge, Tennessee, as the fourth of twelve children. Growing up in the Great Smoky Mountains, Dolly experienced firsthand the hardships of poverty. Despite their meager means, her family always found ways to help neighbors in need, instilling a deep sense of community and compassion in her. These early lessons of kindness and giving became the cornerstone of her philanthropic endeavors.

One of her earliest learnings led to the formation of Parton's most celebrated initiatives, the Imagination Library, a program that mails free books to children from birth until they start school. Inspired by her father, Robert Lee Parton, who never learned to read or write, she recognized the power of literacy in breaking the cycle of poverty and launched the Imagination Library in Sevier County, Tennessee in 1995.

An instant success, the program expanded rapidly. By 2000, it had grown to include the entire state of Tennessee. Today, the Imagination Library operates internationally, providing more than 150 million books to children in the United States, Canada, the United Kingdom, Australia, and Ireland. This initiative has significantly impacted early childhood literacy, earning Parton accolades and deep gratitude from countless families. The Imagination Library is a testament to her belief that education is a fundamental right for every child.

On May 3, 1986, stepping down from a steam train bearing the name of her long-held dream, Parton officially opened Dollywood. Located in Pigeon Forge, Tennessee, the theme park was designed to celebrate the best of life, with "homespun fun." Parton succeeded in bringing family entertainment to her hometown in the mountains.

While Dollywood quickly became a popular tourist destination, its impact on the local economy was profound. The park created thousands of jobs, revitalizing the region and providing much-needed economic stability.

However, her vision for Dollywood extended beyond entertainment and economic growth. The Dollywood Foundation, established shortly after the park's opening, focuses on improving the quality of life in the region. The foundation supports various causes, including scholarships for local high school students, family literacy programs, and community improvement projects. Through these efforts, Parton has entertained millions and uplifted an entire community, creating a legacy of hope and opportunity.

As well as creating lasting legacies, her philanthropy shines brightest during times of crisis.

In 2016, wildfires ravaged the Great Smoky Mountains, devastating homes and businesses. Parton sprang into massive and immediate action. She launched the My People Fund, pledging to donate $1,000 per month for six months to families who lost their homes in the fires. The fund distributed millions of dollars, providing immediate relief and helping families rebuild their lives.

But her commitment to disaster relief extends beyond her home region. She has supported numerous causes, including hurricane relief efforts, COVID-19 research, and flood relief. In each instance, her swift and generous response demonstrates her unwavering dedication to helping others.

She also provides long-term support for those in need, not only addressing a current crisis, but also helping to prevent it from becoming an epidemic. She donates generously to the Dr. Robert F. Thomas Foundation, which provides healthcare services in Sevier County, including prenatal care, pediatric care, and wellness programs. Her contributions have helped residents have access to quality healthcare, regardless of their financial situation.

Parton maintains her love for the arts, performing on global stages late into her 70s (and beyond, we hope), and this love is evident in her support for various cultural initiatives. She funded numerous arts programs, believing in the power of music and storytelling to inspire and heal. She has supported the construction of the Sevier County High School band room and funded music and arts programs across the country. Her contributions have nurtured countless young artists, ensuring the arts remain a vibrant part of community life.

Parton's deep connection to the Smoky Mountains has fostered a lifelong commitment to environmental conservation as well. Through Dollywood and her foundation, she has supported numerous ecological initiatives, including wildlife preservation, reforestation projects, and conservation education programs. Her efforts have helped protect the region's natural beauty, allowing future generations to enjoy the pristine landscapes that shaped her childhood.

Dolly Parton's philanthropic activities reflect her boundless compassion and unwavering commitment to improving the world. Her initiatives in education, economic revitalization, disaster relief, arts and culture, and environmental conservation have created a living legacy that continues to grow and inspire, and one we are certain has the very best chance to become infinite.

But her philanthropy is not just about giving money; it's about giving hope, love, and support to those who need it most. Her ability to connect with people from all walks of life and her genuine desire to make a difference have made her a beloved figure worldwide.

She says, "If you see someone without a smile, give them one of yours."

> **"If you see someone without a smile, give them one of yours."**

Through her philanthropic work, she has given countless smiles, touched innumerable lives, and created a legacy that will endure for generations. Her story is a shining example of how one person's generosity and vision can transform the world, one good deed at a time.

When we learn her story, it is easy to say, "Well that is OK, for her she is rich." The reality is you can be rich and not do all the things she does, or, you can have no money and still make an impact on the world.

Let's take a look at the life of another incredible woman, Maya Angelou.

I've learned that people will forget what you said, people will forget what you did, but people will never forget how you made them feel. —Maya Angelou

---

I've learned that people will forget what you said, people will forget what you did, but people will never forget how you made them feel. —Maya Angelou

---

Maya Angelou, born Marguerite Annie Johnson in 1928, in St. Louis, Missouri, emerged from the depths of poverty and adversity to become one of the most influential voices in American literature and civil rights. While she is best known for her literary prowess, her philanthropic efforts played an equally crucial role in shaping her enduring legacy. Her commitment to giving back has a legacy that continues to inspire and uplift communities worldwide.

Angelou's early years were marked by hardship and instability. After her parents' tumultuous marriage ended in divorce, she and her brother, Bailey, were sent to live with their grandmother in Stamps, Arkansas. The rural South exposed her, for the first time, to the harsh realities of racial segregation and economic deprivation.

Despite these challenges, her grandmother's unwavering faith and community spirit left an indelible mark on her. In this environment, she developed a deep sense of empathy and a desire to help others. Her personal experiences with poverty and injustice fueled a lifelong commitment to philanthropy. But it was when she rose to prominence as a writer and activist that she could fully realize her philanthropic vision.

Her breakthrough came with the publication of her autobiography, *I Know Why the Caged Bird Sings*, in 1969. The book's success catapulted her into the national spotlight, providing a platform for her to advocate for civil rights and social justice. Her powerful voice resonated with millions, and she quickly became a prominent figure in the civil rights movement.

As her influence grew, so did her philanthropic efforts. She believed education was the key to breaking the cycle of poverty and discrimination, and she dedicated much of her time and resources to supporting educational initiatives. One of her earliest philanthropic endeavors was establishing scholarships for underprivileged students at historically black colleges and universities (HBCUs). Her scholarships provided financial support and served as a beacon of hope for countless young people striving to overcome adversity.

In the 1980s, she expanded her philanthropic activities by founding several community centers in underserved neighborhoods. These centers offered various services, including tutoring, vocational training, and counselling. She understood that education alone was insufficient; people needed holistic support to thrive. The community centers became safe havens where individuals could access resources, find mentorship, and build a sense of community.

One of the most impactful centers was the Maya Angelou Community Center in Winston-Salem, North Carolina, where she later settled. This center provided after-school programs for children, adult literacy classes, and job placement services. She visited the center often and became deeply involved in its activities, speaking with participants and offering encouragement. Her presence and personal investment in these initiatives inspired many to pursue their dreams despite the obstacles they faced.

A staunch advocate for women's rights, Angelou worked tirelessly to support organizations dedicated to empowering women and children. She collaborated with groups like the Women's Rights Movement and the Children's Defense Fund, using her influence to raise awareness and money for their causes. Her poetry and speeches often highlighted women's struggles and triumphs, giving a voice to those who had been silenced.

One of her notable contributions was her work with the United Negro College Fund (UNCF). Because of her passionate advocacy and fundraising efforts, she helped the UNCF provide scholarships and support services to thousands of African American students. Her famous stance—"When you learn, teach. When you get, give."—became a guiding principle for the organization and underscored her belief in the transformative power of education.

Because of her profile, now at a global level, Angelou's travels exposed her to dimensions of poverty and injustice on an international scale, and she felt a profound responsibility to act. Extending her philanthropy beyond the United States, she was deeply committed to humanitarian causes, wherever they may be. In the 1990s, she partnered with international organizations like UNICEF and Amnesty International to advocate for children's and human rights. She participated in numerous campaigns to raise awareness about issues such as child labor, human trafficking, and access to education in developing countries. Her eloquence and moral authority brought global attention to these critical issues, and her efforts helped mobilize support and resources for vulnerable populations.

Maya Angelou's philanthropic endeavors created a living legacy that continues to inspire and uplift, even after her death in 2014. Her scholarships have enabled countless students to pursue higher education and achieve their dreams. The community centers she established remain vital resources for individuals seeking support and empowerment. Her advocacy for women and children has left an indelible mark on the fight for gender equality and social justice. In addition to her direct philanthropic activities, her writing and public speaking inspired generations of activists, educators, and philanthropists. Her works are taught in schools worldwide, and her messages of resilience, compassion, and hope resonate with people from all walks of life. Through her words and deeds, Maya Angelou demonstrated that one person can make a profound difference in the world no matter how humble their beginnings.

Ultimately, her life was a testament to the power of resilience, empathy, and action. Angelou's story reminds us that true greatness lies in personal achievement and the ability to uplift others and leave a lasting legacy of kindness and justice.

Throughout these stories of the legacy created by people, we can all see small acts that we can replicate. If we act consistently, even in a small way, then we can create our own living legacy.

We want to share one more inspiring story: Malala Yousafzai.

I tell my story not because it is unique, but because it is the story of many girls.
—Malala Yousafzai

Malala Yousafzai was born on July 12, 1997, in the Swat Valley of Pakistan. This region was once known for its natural beauty but later became infamous due to the rise of the Taliban. Her father, Ziauddin Yousafzai, was a passionate educator who ran a chain of regional schools. From an early age, a love for learning and a determination to fight for education rights was instilled within her.

Growing up, she witnessed the increasing influence of the Taliban, who imposed strict regulations that mainly affected girls' access to education and, in 2007, when she was 10 years old, they began to enforce bans on girls attending school.

Despite the threats and dangers, Malala and her father were undeterred.

They continued to advocate for education, with Malala writing a blog under a pseudonym for the BBC, detailing life under Taliban rule and her desire to attend school.

On October 9, 2012, her life changed forever.

While riding the bus home from school, she was targeted and shot by a Taliban gunman. The bullet struck her head, critically injuring her. The attack sparked international outrage and brought attention to the plight of millions of children denied education around the world. She was airlifted to the United Kingdom for treatment, where she made a miraculous recovery.

Her situation resonated globally, transforming her into a symbol of resistance against oppression. Despite the trauma and the ongoing threats to her life, her resolve only strengthened. She understood that her survival was not only a personal triumph but also a call to action for global education rights.

In 2013, and alongside her father, they co-founded the Malala Fund, a nonprofit organization dedicated to ensuring girls around the world have access to 12 years of free, safe, and quality education.

The fund focuses on advocacy, amplifying the voices of young girls, and supporting local education activists. It operates on the principle that empowering girls through education can transform communities and break the cycle of poverty.

Although the initial efforts of the nonprofit were directed toward raising awareness and funds, following her first public appearance after the attack, at the United Nations on her sixteenth birthday, she delivered a profoundly powerful speech calling on world leaders to provide education for all children. This speech marked the beginning of her role as a global advocate for education.

The Malala Fund's impact has been profound and far-reaching. One of its key initiatives is the Gulmakai Network, named after her pseudonym when she wrote her BBC blog. This network supports local advocates in countries like Pakistan, Afghanistan, Nigeria, and India, where girls face significant barriers to education. These advocates work on the ground, addressing specific community challenges and implementing programs to increase girls' school enrollment and retention rates.

In Pakistan, the fund has worked to rebuild and expand schools, especially in areas affected by conflict. It has partnered with local organizations to provide scholarships and teacher training, ensuring that girls receive a quality education. The fund also supported community-based education in Afghanistan, bringing learning opportunities to remote and underserved areas where formal schools are inaccessible.

And in Nigeria, the focus has been on regions affected by the Boko Haram insurgency, which has targeted schools and kidnapped students. The fund collaborates with local groups to provide safe learning environments and psycho-social support for girls who have been traumatized by violence. These efforts have helped girls return to school and advocated for their right to education in national and international forums.

Malala's advocacy goes beyond grassroots initiatives. She has consistently engaged with global leaders, urging them to prioritize education in their policies and funding. In 2014, at 17 years old, she became the youngest-ever recipient of the Nobel Peace Prize. This recognition amplified her voice, allowing her to advocate more effectively on international platforms.

The Malala Fund has successfully lobbied for increased funding for education, particularly in conflict zones. It has also influenced policy changes, such as the Global Partnership for Education's replenishment, which saw billions of dollars committed to improving education systems in developing countries.

In addition to her famous address at the United Nations, she has also spoken to the World Bank and various governments, reminding them of their commitments to the Sustainable Development Goals, particularly Goal 4: Quality Education for All.

One of her most significant legacies is the inspiration she provides to young people worldwide. She has become a role model, showing that age and gender are not barriers to making a difference. Through her speeches, books, and public appearances, she encourages the youth of today to stand up for their rights and pursue their dreams, regardless of the obstacles.

Her autobiography, *I Am Malala*, has been translated into numerous languages, spreading her message to a global audience. The book narrates her journey and highlights the broader issues of education and women's rights. It has become a source of inspiration for students, educators, and activists, igniting a passion for change.

Today, she relentlessly continues to champion the cause of education from her base in the United Kingdom, where she graduated from Oxford University with a degree in Philosophy, Politics, and Economics. Her academic achievements are a testament to her belief in the transformative power of education. She remains actively involved in the Malala Fund's initiatives, regularly visiting projects and meeting with the girls whose lives have been impacted by the organization's work.

Her legacy is more than the schools built, the policies changed, and the funds raised. It is in the countless lives she has touched, the voices she has amplified, and the hope she has instilled in girls around the world. Her story is a powerful reminder that one person's courage and determination can ignite a global movement for change.

Malala Yousafzai has created a living legacy that transcends borders and generations.

From the valleys of Swat to the halls of the United Nations, her journey is a beacon of hope for those fighting for education and equality. Through the Malala Fund, she has empowered millions of girls to pursue their dreams, ensuring that her impact will be felt for years to come.

Her life and work epitomize the belief that education is not only a right but also a powerful catalyst for a better world.

These stories of three incredible women give us ideas and insight into the legacy projects we want in our lives and what we can do to make a difference, big or small.

The key to a living legacy is a commitment to consistency.

When we act with commitment, and do so consistently, we can create our legacy.

When we act with commitment, and do so consistently, we can create our legacy. We will create a living legacy, so let us all make sure it is a good one of real value. It is our thoughts and actions that dictate our legacy. We owe it to ourselves to act, both on purpose and, with purpose, throughout our lives. If you have not done so before, now is the best time to start.

We owe it to ourselves to act, both on purpose and, with purpose, throughout our lives.

We'll close this chapter with wisdom from Dolly Parton. "If your actions create a legacy that inspires others to dream more, learn more, do more and become more, then, you are an excellent leader."

Well said Dolly! The actions you take today position you to create a living legacy, just like these amazing women.

CHAPTER 9

PRINCIPLE 2: GIVE WHAT YOU CAN AFFORD WHEN YOU CAN AFFORD IT – THE INFINITE LEGACY TRIO OF TIME, TALENT, AND TREASURE

In the world of philanthropy, the trio of "time, talent, and treasure" embodies the multifaceted nature of giving. It goes beyond donations and highlights the significance of offering other significant ways of building a legacy including giving one's time as well as unique skills to charitable causes.

Time

Time, often referred to as the most precious commodity, holds a special place in charitable endeavors. Warren Buffett, the well-known investor and philanthropist, emphasizes this with various iterations of the same sentiment: He can buy anything, but he cannot buy more time. With this in mind, we recognize that one of the most precious things we can give to someone is our time.

Volunteering exemplifies an individual's dedication to causes promoting community involvement and social issues.

Volunteering exemplifies an individual's dedication to causes promoting community involvement and social issues.

Seen as a form of currency, time plays an important role in charitable initiatives globally. To quote Nobel laureate Desmond Tutu; "Do your little bit of good where you are; it's those little bits of good put together that overwhelm the world." Volunteering transcends borders by fostering a sense of unity and shared responsibility in tackling important issues affecting people worldwide.

According to the United Nations Volunteers (UNV) program, volunteers collectively contribute more than 1 billion hours of service annually across 140 countries. The worldwide dedication to volunteer work highlights its role in developing communities and aiding causes such as supporting education projects in remote areas and delivering healthcare services in regions affected by conflict and natural disasters. Giving time to these efforts leads to numerous benefits to help the less fortunate.

Justdiggit is a notprofit organization that recognizes that global warming is moving in fast. In their words, the Earth is "drying up," and they have taken it upon themselves to reverse it. In addition to this, they also recognize that this is a pressing matter, and there is only one decade to stop the warming.

They know it's necessary to keep the global temperature increase below 2°C to stop irreversible damage to the planet that sustains all of us, and that we will need to act together, and to act with urgency, to be able to achieve this.

They cite the challenge as climate change, they have chosen the place as Africa, and have identified the solution as nature. Based on research by the Nature Conservancy and in partnership with the Doris Duke Foundation, 37 percent of the climate problem can be solved by applying nature-based solutions. At a local level, regreening barren land and utilizing the time of people living in the hardest hit communities can lead to a huge impact.

Let's take a closer look at how the investment of time can reap significant dividends.

Justdiggit's headline technique involves nothing more than a simple hand tool that the local population have almost unlimited access to, and the time to dig a bund. These bunds, or "earth smiles" as they are known on social media, capture rainwater that would otherwise run off the compacted soil, giving it more time to enter the local water table and restore the natural balance.

Over just a period of weeks following the creation of bunds, seeds that were already in the soil get a chance to sprout, and eventually allow the area to grow green, lush and cool.

Another method, "treecovery" (or Farmer Managed Natural Regeneration), is a process that involves the selective pruning and protection of seemingly lifeless stumps, which provides the right care to allow these trees to grow again.

Combine these two initiatives with the creation of Grass Seed Banks, which allow the women of the Maasai, to grow, harvest, and sell grass (hay) and seeds, it has led to what essentially is on an individual level, a small investment of time, to have a global impact.

With more than 450,000 earth smiles dug and 18.7 million trees recovered, Justdiggit has restored more than 430,000 hectares of land by retaining 6.6 billion liters of water in 2023 alone.

Our time begins at birth and ends on this earth with death. For most, it is about 25,000 days. Our time is precious and cannot be stored up like grain in a barn. Once a moment passes it is gone forever. Assisting individuals and organizations is a way to share our personal time and when enough of us do this, the impact can be vast.

> **Our time is precious and cannot be stored up like grain in a barn.**

Your gift of time is unique because you are the only one who can give it, but like Justdiggit has recognized, we understand that the gift of time can be the beginning of a legacy that changes the world around us.

To find out more about this amazing initiative go to www.justdiggit.org.

Talent

When it comes to talent, the idea of using skills for good is deeply felt in philanthropy. Melinda Gates, co-chair of the Bill & Melinda Gates Foundation, recognizes that everyone can make a difference through their time, talents, or resources. This underscores the importance of a variety of skills in tackling issues.

> **When it comes to talent, the idea of using skills for good is deeply felt in philanthropy.**

According to International Labour Organization's manual on the measurement of volunteer work, 20 million people engage in volunteering based on their skills each year showing an interest in using expertise to address social challenges. Skill-based volunteering, where individuals provide knowledge to nonprofits has become an aspect of modern philanthropy. A study by LinkedIn indicates that 89 percent of professionals believe that volunteering helps improve their job-related skills highlighting the connection between growth and social impact.

Whether you prefer him as a military general on a giant worm-infested Sand Planet, a wheelchair bound telekinetically enhanced professor, or in the eyes of two out of three of the authors of this book, the best starship captain in the federation, Patrick Stewart has had a long, wide reaching and illustrious career.

The star of stage and screen almost remained unknown, and as recalled in his memoir *Making It So*, if it wasn't for the talent of Mr. Cecil Dormand, an extraordinary English teacher, the bridge of the USS Enterprise would have looked very different indeed.

When Stewart was 11 years old, he had the chance to take the 11+ exam, a pivotal test in the English education system that determined whether a student would advance to a grammar school, considered the more prestigious option, or attend a secondary modern school. However, instead of sitting for the exam, Stewart spent his time wandering the hills near his hometown of Mirfield in West Yorkshire. Even if he had taken the test, Stewart doubted he would have passed and never envisioned himself as a grammar school student.

This decision led him to a secondary modern school where he encountered Cecil "Cec" Dormand, an English teacher who would profoundly shape his future. From the very first moment Dormand had Stewart recite Shakespeare's line, "I have possessed your grace of what I purpose," it was clear that Stewart felt an immediate and deep connection to something new and thrilling. Dormand, who also served as his form master, had a teaching style that was both relaxed and engaging. He was funny, provocative, and above all, passionate about his subject, making literature feel alive and relevant.

Dormand quickly recognized Stewart's love for stories and his desire to escape the difficulties of his home life, which was overshadowed by an abusive father. He brought literature and language to life, offering Stewart a refuge in the world of fiction. That same year, Dormand cast Stewart in a play alongside adults, many of whom were teachers. Despite having no prior acting experience, Stewart found himself feeling completely at ease on stage, drawing on the confidence Dormand had instilled in him.

Not long after, Stewart was offered the chance to attend an eight-day residential drama course at Calder High School during the Easter break. This opportunity was later revealed to have been championed—and perhaps even funded—by Dormand, marking the first time Stewart received formal acting training.

A few days before leaving school at the age of 15, Dormand asked Stewart if he had ever considered pursuing acting as a career. The idea seemed laughable to Stewart at the time, but it planted a seed. Two years later, Stewart was accepted into the Bristol Old Vic Theatre School on a scholarship—a rare achievement typically reserved for Oxbridge students. His acceptance was undoubtedly bolstered by a powerful letter of recommendation from Dormand.

Years later, Stewart, serving as chancellor of the University of Huddersfield, was able to express his gratitude by awarding

Dormand an honorary degree. He further honored Dormand by inviting him to a luncheon celebrating Stewart's knighthood, an event where Dormand jokingly pondered, "What the heck am I going to call him now? For decades, he called me Sir!"

Dormand passed away at the age of 96, leaving behind a legacy of transforming simple text into a world of imaginative escape and nurturing the talents of countless students. Reflecting on Dormand's influence, Stewart remarked, "He saved me when I was a boy and my education was failing. He has, without a doubt, been the most significant person in my life. If I had not met Cec, what would have happened to me? I am forever grateful for his belief in me. Rest in peace, Sir."

Treasure

Financial contributions remain a cornerstone of charitable endeavors, facilitating the implementation of vital programs and initiatives. Andrew Carnegie once famously stated that it is an obligation for those with wealth to use it for the benefit of the community during their lifetime. Donations from philanthropists play a role in expanding the impact and bringing about changes in various areas.

That said, the common citizen can impact individual lives by offering resources according to their means. One way to look at this notion, which is in line with Principle 2, is to "give from your saucer, not your cup." This means that as your cup overflows with some level of prosperity, you should give from that saucer that it flows into. As one becomes more successful and has a larger cup, more overflows from that cup into the saucer; therefore, it is easy to give more from a larger saucer. Whether you are a blue-collar worker, millionaire, or billionaire, we can all give freely from our saucer if we choose to do so.

> **That said, the common citizen can impact individual lives by offering resources according to their means.**

The global landscape of philanthropy has experienced growth with emerging economies taking on increasingly important roles. The World Giving Index highlights countries such as Indonesia, Kenya, and Myanmar where individual giving as a percentage of GDP is growing and there is an inclination toward generosity and empathy in these and other developing nations. Data from Giving USA Foundation's Annual Report demonstrate the influence of contributions with charitable donations in the United States reaching $449.64 billion in 2019. These funds contribute to causes such as education, healthcare, and disaster relief emphasizing the role of financial support in promoting societal well-being.

Giving also benefits the giver. In a publication by Elizabeth W. Dunn, Lara B. Aknin, and Michael I. Norton in *Science*, they discovered that spending money on others promotes happiness.

In their publication, they explore the relationship between how people spend their money and their overall happiness. Their research presents compelling evidence that the act of spending money on others, referred to as prosocial spending, can lead to greater happiness compared to spending money on oneself. Through a series of studies, the authors demonstrate that individuals who allocate their financial resources toward others experience enhanced emotional well-being, highlighting that the way money is spent can be as important as the amount of money one earns. This work challenges the traditional notion that personal spending brings the most satisfaction, suggesting instead that generosity and the social connections it fosters are key contributors to happiness.

The study suggests that once basic needs are met, spending money on others as part of your spending mix is positive for your happiness. Specifically, participants were given an envelope containing a small sum of money and told to spend it within 24 hours. Half of them were required to spend the money on themselves (e.g., by paying a bill or buying a treat), and the other half were required to spend it on others (e.g., by buying a present or donating the money to charity). The results were clear: subjects in the second group reported greater happiness than those in the first.

Other studies by Harvard Business School (2010) have suggested that there is a positive connection between giving to charity and subjective well-being. The astonishing conclusion was that, on average, "donating to charity has a similar relationship to happiness as a doubling of household income."

The story of married couple Julia Wise and Jeff Kaufman illustrate this point well. Wise and Kaufman both individually felt compelled to give back, believing that generosity enriched others' lives as well as their own. When they married, they committed to donating a portion of their income to charities. As reported in *Quartz*, Wise and Kaufman earned a combined income of nearly $245,000 in 2013 and lived on $15,280 (not including taxes and savings)—only 6.25% of their income.

So, what did they do with the rest of their income, which was just under $100,000? The couple decided to donate that portion to charity. Impressively, this act of generosity wasn't a one-time occurrence; they have maintained a similar level of charitable giving each year since 2008, reflecting their deep commitment to philanthropy and frugal living. In sum, according to a detailed table on Kaufman's website, the couple has donated nearly $2.2 million as of 2023 to various charities, even as their family has grown to include three children. They pledged to donate 30 percent of their income, but their actual donations are closer to 50 percent.

We constantly overestimate the impact income will have on our happiness levels. People who know Wise and Kaufman describe them "as some of the happiest people they know." In an article on Project BOLD Life, they said "they would not have things any other way." You may not currently be able to gift 30-50 percent of your income to others. What you can do is make a start and seek to increase it over time.

Studies show that taking a cut in income makes only a small difference to your overall happiness. This is because of the things that will remain regardless of income such as family and friendships.

For many people, their ability to give time, talent, and treasure evolves over time and lands in a space that is relevant to where they are at that period in their life. We know someone who as a young man in his 20s had no money to speak of and didn't have any specialized talent to contribute to a nonprofit organization. But he did have time. And so, he volunteered his time once a week to the Big Brothers program in the United States. Big Brothers and Big

Sisters is an organization that pairs up young boys and girls who have no adult role models in their life. The Big Brother or Big Sister connects with their "little brother" or "little sister" once a week to talk and do activities together. Our friend found this to be a great way to contribute to the community in a way that he could do at the time.

Later, when he started to achieve some success in business, he joined a local Rotary Club to contribute his time and his developing talents to various community causes. While in Rotary, he met a board member for a local children's center in the community. Given his background in Big Brothers and his involvement in Rotary, he was invited to be a board member for the children's center.

Now, he was in a position to provide some time, his acquired talent in running an organization, and some treasure in the form of financial contributions to the larger organization.

Later, he was invited to be on the Board of Trustees for a local university where he was able to provide his time, talent, and treasure regularly. At this point in his career, he was also able to contribute a substantial sum of money to another local children's program that was able to build a library in his family name.

As you can see in our friend's story, his contribution of time, talent, and treasure was an evolution over 45 years. Not everyone will have the same trajectory and few of us will be able to fund a library, but that's not the message from this story. The message is that wherever we are in our journey of life, we can contribute what we are able to contribute given where we are in that journey. We believe that we should all give from our saucer, not our cup. As our cup overflows and we find that we have more resources, we should give freely from that overflowing cup by offering our time, our talent, and/or our treasure— whatever has overflowed from our life. This is a great metaphor for the legacy we can leave in the world.

As our cup overflows and we find that we have more resources, we should give freely from that overflowing cup by offering our time, our talent, and/or our treasure— whatever has overflowed from our life.

CHAPTER 10

PRINCIPLE 2: GIVE WHAT YOU CAN AFFORD WHEN YOU CAN AFFORD IT – GIFTING YOUR TIME, TALENT, AND TREASURE

While it is possible to create an Infinite Legacy based on only one of the trio, something amazing happens when we start combining two or all three of these cornerstones.

Time with treasure allows the compounded impact of actions to be multiplied with effective tools. Talent and treasure allow for a wider reach of our skills. And where time and talent come together, we not only pass on a new skill, but also create an accomplished user of those skills, who in turn will now have the ability to teach others.

However, it is when all three—time, talent, and treasure—combine that something magical happens.

Roberto Clemente, the first Latin American baseball player to achieve 3,000 hits, was a Hall of Famer renowned for his incredible talent on the field and also for his deep commitment to humanitarian efforts. Throughout his illustrious career, Clemente earned four batting titles, 12 Gold Glove Awards, and recognition as the National League's Most Valuable Player in 1966. As a 15-time All-Star, he played a pivotal role in leading the Pittsburgh Pirates to two World Series championships, even earning the title of Most Valuable Player in the 1971 World Series at 37 years old.

Clemente's powerful swing, speed, and exceptional throwing arm made him a legend in baseball, but his legacy extended far beyond the ballpark. He was equally admired for his compassion, charitable work, and his dedication to advocating for social and economic justice.

Believing that baseball could be a force for positive change in the lives of Puerto Rican children, much like it had been for him, Clemente frequently brought baseballs and gloves to young fans and organized clinics across the island. These clinics, which reached thousands of children, especially those from underprivileged backgrounds, were about more than just teaching the game. As Clemente put it:

"I gather the kids and talk about the importance of sports, being a good citizen, and showing respect for their parents… Then we hit the field, where I teach them some of the finer points of playing baseball."

Clemente's dedication to both his sport and his community made him a true role model, whose influence continues to be felt long after his passing. Like our friend in the previous story, he is a standout example of a person who created a legacy that consisted of all three of the Infinite Legacy Trio. He gave his time, his talent, and his treasure.

Throughout his baseball career, he continued to work on what he considered to be his ultimate legacy and sought land and investors for what he called "the biggest ambition in my life", a "sports city" where Puerto Rican children of all classes could live for short periods of time and learn various sports. This ambition was widely reported during his lifetime as he sought land and investors to make the project a reality.

To understand how one person can have such a broad and wide-reaching vision on the legacy they can leave, it often helps to look at their journey.

After signing a big-league contract for the Pittsburgh Pirates as a young man, Clemente arrived in the United States to an off-season training camp where he experienced the effects of the Jim Crow segregation laws. These were a set of state and local laws introduced in the Southern United States in the late nineteenth and early twentieth centuries that enforced racial segregation.

Clemente faced pervasive racial discrimination throughout his career in the United States, especially during his early years. He often found himself segregated from his white teammates, forced into separate lodging, and denied access to certain restaurants and entertainment venues. This segregation extended to team events, where he was excluded from activities such as the team golf tournament and other gatherings. Additionally, the media frequently disrespected his Puerto Rican heritage by Anglicizing his name to "Bob" or "Bobby" and mocking his accent by printing his quotes phonetically.

Clemente's commitment to equality was unwavering, and he was deeply influenced by Martin Luther King Jr., whom he considered a personal hero. The two met multiple times, and Clemente even hosted King at his farm in Puerto Rico. After King's assassination in 1968, Clemente insisted that the Pittsburgh Pirates and the Houston Astros postpone their season-opening series until after King's burial, reflecting his deep commitment to civil rights.

In the final season of his career, after reaching the milestone of 3,000 hits, Clemente traveled to Nicaragua with his wife, Vera, to manage a Puerto Rican team in the world amateur baseball championships. Clemente's humanitarian spirit was evident as he and Vera spent time with local children, offering them financial support and even arranging for one boy to travel to the United States for prosthetic legs.

A few weeks after their return to Puerto Rico, a catastrophic earthquake struck Nicaragua. Deeply moved by the disaster, Clemente quickly organized a relief effort. He tirelessly sought donations, appearing on television and going door-to-door in affluent neighborhoods, even during the Christmas holiday, to gather supplies for the victims. His efforts resulted in more than $150,000 in donations and 26 tons of food, clothing, and medicine.

Tragically, on New Year's Eve 1972, Clemente decided to accompany a shipment of supplies to Nicaragua after hearing that corrupt officials were diverting the aid. The overloaded plane crashed shortly after takeoff, killing all aboard. Clemente's body was never recovered.

While the world lost a baseball legend, Clemente's legacy as a humanitarian lives on. His name graces schools, parks, and bridges from Puerto Rico to Pittsburgh, and even in Germany. The Puerto Rican government honored his dream by establishing the Roberto Clemente Sports City, which has benefited more than a million children, including future Major League Baseball stars.

Every year on September 15th, during National Hispanic Heritage Month, Major League Baseball celebrates Roberto Clemente Day. The Roberto Clemente Award is also presented annually to a player who best exemplifies the values Clemente stood for:

sportsmanship, community involvement, and contributions to their team. His sons continue to carry on his charitable work through the Roberto Clemente Foundation, ensuring that his spirit of giving endures.

Clemente's Legacy lives on infinitely, not because that is how he designed it. It lives on because of his passion to make an impact in the world. He had a passion to take his time, his talent and his treasure and make it a genuine force for good in areas where he had a real emotional connection.

We are all born with time. Many of us have natural talents, and we develop those and further talents over time. Some of us are lucky to have, earn, or acquire some level of treasure that we are prepared to donate to others for a greater good than to spend it on ourselves.

To create your legacy, you only need one of these cornerstones. You can create a legacy based on just your time, just your talent, or just your treasure. The choice is yours and our journey through life gives us many opportunities to do just that.

It is common for us all to delay all thoughts of the legacy that we will create. Many people spend their time surviving and working hard from one day to the next with very little thought of legacy or a legacy project. We want to show that everyone can turn their whole life into a legacy project with a little thought and planning.

Part of what gets in the way of our legacy project is the assumption that legacy will take too much of our time, or that we don't have what it takes to build a legacy, or that legacy costs money and we just do not have spare money in our lives. The truth is our life is full of opportunities to create a legacy, and even more so, a legacy project. We just need to know how.

Legacy has three cornerstones, The Infinite Legacy Trio. These cornerstones are the building blocks for our legacy project. They allow us to decide how we can start, continue, and leave legacy projects in our life.

The reality is, we will often be presented with potential legacy options in our lifetime. Some will start but never be completed, some will never start, and some will be realized. Knowing that the path to legacy is full of failure should excite us to look for legacy opportunities as often as we can.

By understanding the three cornerstones, we can identify when we have either deliberately or accidently started a legacy project. The cornerstones are gifts from us to the world. In legacy we can either give our time, our talent, or our treasure and often we will give more than just one to any specific project; it is only when we run short of one of these three resources, in the absence of at least one of the other two, that our project fails or falters.

If our legacy has a strong base in our "Why," and is a passion of ours, then we will be motivated to continue more so than if it were a project that we are less emotional about. Sometimes we give time talent and treasure to somebody else's passion. With other people's passion, we will withdraw more quickly if we come under pressure elsewhere for our time, our talent, or our treasure. Other times we run out despite our best efforts to continue.

Typically, we will start our personal passion legacy project by investing time. Ironically, we begin by giving this freely, like we have an unlimited amount of it; however, in many ways time is the most precious resource of all because we don't know how much of it we will get to spend.

Talent is limited, as it is often linked to time, it can be developed by us over many years, but this takes the investment of our own personal efforts, and energy in learning.

Treasure, despite being the one that is normally the last to arrive, ultimately is unlimited (within reason)—once we know how, we can always earn more money.

In the context of Infinite Legacy, time is simply us investing seconds, minutes, and hours into developing a legacy project. This could be helping a community project, writing a book, or planting a tree. All of these things take time and typically will require a consistent effort over a long period for them to turn into an Infinite Legacy.

We can, however, invest a small amount of time that can change people's lives around us and create a ripple effect that ultimately leaves a lasting legacy for one person, one family, or one community.

When we invest our talents, we are adding to time spent, multiplying its impact by bringing our talent to help others.

Everyone has a talent. Talent alone is not enough to build an Infinite Legacy. We need to add time to this and the dedication to succeed. Often the very process that allowed us to develop our talent in the first place is the same process we apply to our legacy project.

Our treasure is defined as many things, the most obvious being money. It can also be our influence, our collections, or our possessions which we can gift to a legacy project.

Adding treasure to your own legacy project can be a standalone act, but when combined with time and talent, this simple addition can quickly help create an Infinite Legacy.

The trio of time, talent, and treasure symbolizes the multifaceted nature of philanthropy by stressing the ways individuals can contribute to enhancing society through volunteer work, utilizing skills, and providing assistance within their community. In this way, people collectively drive positive change and address critical social needs. As Mahatma Gandhi once said; "The best way to find yourself is to lose yourself in the service of others." By adopting this philosophy people can use their abilities to make a lasting difference and promote a fairer and kinder world.

The trio of time, talent, and treasure symbolizes the multifaceted nature of philanthropy by stressing the ways individuals can contribute to enhancing society.

Regardless of whatever you can currently afford to give—time, talent, or treasure—we all can create an Infinite Legacy.

"If you have a chance to accomplish something that will make things better for people coming behind you, and you don't do that, you are wasting your time on this Earth." —Roberto Clemente

CHAPTER 11

PRINCIPLE 2: GIVE WHAT YOU CAN AFFORD WHEN YOU CAN AFFORD IT – THE EVOLUTION OF LEAVING A LEGACY

"Do what you can, with what you have, where you are." This sentiment by former United States President Theodore Roosevelt suggests how a legacy can grow and evolve over time.

At the various stages of our legacy development, we may need to lean on our time, talent, and treasure, or combinations of all three, differently. The most precious of the Infinite Legacy Trio is time. While we can continually improve our talent (Einstein correctly said, "once you stop learning you start dying") and we can always improve our treasure, we cannot develop or purchase more time.

It is ironic then, that in the beginning, time is the easiest commodity to use to start developing your own legacy. Visit any charitable shop over the weekend and you will see it staffed by the younger generation who are looking to give back to worthwhile causes.

Time seems limitless when you are young. We've heard of projects where patches of wasteland are turned into community gardens, the elderly are offered companionship, and the most vulnerable animals are exercised and cared for. None of this takes talent or in any way treasure. It is simply an investment of time.

The great news for legacy building therefore is that we can have an impact from a very early age. We can begin our own legacy creation with little more than compassion and a willingness to donate our time. We are not saying for a moment that the younger generation are not talented; we are saying that the abundant commodity they have to give is time.

> **We can begin our own legacy creation with little more than compassion and a willingness to donate our time.**

As we move forward in our lives, we develop skills. In some cases, these are professional skills that we have studied toward; in other cases, these are vocational skills that we have developed during our extracurricular and social time. Our legacies can be based on our talent, finding a worthwhile challenge that our skillset can solve and choosing to build a legacy around that.

You can combine time and talent and choose to teach a skill to those less fortunate that wouldn't have had the opportunity otherwise, or you can apply your professional knowledge to assist an existing nongovernmental organization (NGO), or charity navigate the world of business more effectively.

Finally, we come to treasure. For those that have built a life with a capacity of abundance and are often still actively involved in the day to day running of their business interests, donating treasure allows for the opportunity to make a difference with little or no investment of time and talent.

Take the Bill & Melinda Gate Foundation as an example.

Is Bill Gates talented? Undoubtably, you could argue that he has had more of an impact on modern-day life that any other figure in the last 100 year. We are, let's not forget, writing this book on a Microsoft program.

Can Bill Gates single-handedly rid the world of malaria?

Well, we wouldn't bet against him, but with all the investment of time and talent that he could muster, we would have to give him very steep odds as this simply isn't his field of expertise. This is why Bill and Melinda have to date donated more than $36 billion to recruiting and applying the best and brightest in the field of disease eradication and control to the task at hand. They had a vision and the treasure to do something about it, so they are renumerating others who hold the time and talent to leave a lasting legacy.

Their vision for the foundation is so strong: "Our mission is to create a world where every person has the opportunity to live a healthy, productive life."

Others with treasure have committed to helping them achieve this ambitious vision, including Warren Buffett, who committed to donating half of his Berkshire shares to the foundation with an estimated value of between $30-45 billion.

We cannot help but feel that the most rewarding legacy to build would be one that reflected all three foundation cornerstones of time, talent, and treasure. With all three involved, you would enjoy the time investment, be challenged by the application of your talent, and be rewarded when you see others benefiting from your treasure.

This could be a passionate local artist running a project to create a community piece, where they teach the skills, provide the materials, and ultimately introduce a whole new audience to their passion, all while enhancing the environment around them.

Or it could be a committed and talented Chief Financial Officer, who takes a position as a trustee of a charity with a focus on a subject close to their hearts, using their professional time, talent, and treasure to ensure the best use of funds.

Inevitably, as we progress through our lives, we will have an abundance or shortage of each of these. The real key to legacy building is to find one, where you can start right away, using what you have in surplus, and to make sure that as your personal situation develops, your legacy continues to grow alongside your own journey.

One remarkable story of a person whose legacy evolved from giving time, to giving talent, and finally giving money is that of Andrew Carnegie, the famous industrialist and philanthropist and someone we have already mentioned multiple times.

Andrew Carnegie was born in 1835 in Dunfermline, Scotland. His family emigrated to the United States when he was 13 years old, settling near Pittsburgh, Pennsylvania. Carnegie began his career working as a bobbin boy in a cotton factory, then as a telegraph messenger, and later as a telegraph operator. As a young man, he demonstrated a strong work ethic and a willingness to learn, which led to his advancement in the Pennsylvania Railroad Company. During these early years, Carnegie volunteered his time to help the less fortunate, understanding the struggles of poverty firsthand.

As he gained experience and knowledge in the railroad industry, Carnegie began to invest his earnings in various ventures, including ironworks and bridge building. His talent for business and strategic investments helped him amass a substantial fortune. Recognizing the importance of education and self-improvement, Carnegie used his talents to establish numerous educational initiatives. He funded the creation of public libraries, believing that access to knowledge was crucial for personal and societal advancement. By the time he was 35, Carnegie had dedicated significant time and talent to promoting education and literacy.

In the later stages of his life, Andrew Carnegie's focus shifted from giving time and talent to giving treasure. He sold his steel company to J.P. Morgan for $480 million in 1901, which was an astronomical sum at the time. Carnegie then dedicated the rest of his life to philanthropy, distributing his wealth to various causes. He established the Carnegie Corporation of New York, the Carnegie Endowment for International Peace, the Carnegie Institution for Science, and many other foundations and trusts.

Andrew Carnegie's philosophy on philanthropy was profoundly expressed in his seminal book, *The Gospel of Wealth*. In this influential work, Carnegie asserted that the wealthy bear a significant moral responsibility to use their fortunes for the greater good of society.

He believed that those with great wealth should act as stewards of their riches, dedicating their resources to initiatives that uplift the less fortunate and foster the welfare and happiness of the broader community.

Carnegie's vision was not simply about charity, but also about strategically investing in causes that would empower individuals and promote long-term societal progress. His essay laid the foundation for modern philanthropy, emphasizing that the true measure of wealth lies not in the accumulation of riches, but in their effective use to improve the human condition. He believed in using his money to create opportunities for others, rather than simply giving handouts.

Andrew Carnegie's legacy is vast and enduring. His contributions to education and scientific research continue to benefit society today. The numerous libraries he funded provided countless individuals with the resources to educate themselves and improve their circumstances. His endowments support ongoing research and development in various fields, contributing to global progress.

Carnegie's journey from a poor immigrant to one of the richest men in the world, and then to a philanthropist who gave away most of his fortune, is a powerful example of how one's legacy can develop and expand over a lifetime. His transition from giving time, to talent, and finally treasure, left an indelible mark on the world, and for us, serves as a perfect example of the evolution of a legacy.

CHAPTER 12
PRINCIPLE 3: BE GUIDED BY YOUR PASSION – FIND YOUR PASSION

As a teenager, Mesba Ahmed was obsessed with football (known as soccer in the United States). He grew up as a British Asian boy on the Lisson Green Estate, an area plagued by high-crime rates yet located near the world-famous Lord's Cricket Ground. Despite being so close to the renowned sporting venue, he and his friends had nowhere to play their games.

Speaking to the British newspaper, *The Evening Standard*, he said, "We had to use the streets and pavements of the estate as our football pitch[1], despite the fact that we lived in the heart of wealthy St John's Wood." He went on to say, "Garage doors doubled as goals, coats and jumpers were propped up to make the other goal and when cars came we had to quickly stop the game to let them by." He saw this as a challenge for the youth of Asian communities.

Despite the constant promise of change from the ever-changing portfolio of local officials, more than a decade on from the birth

---
[1] A pitch is referred to as a field in some countries.

of his first son, in 1999, Ahmed had realized nothing had changed and decided to do something about it. He wanted things to be different for his son, and his friends, so began coaching young people from the estate on a rundown, uneven, and some may say, dangerous piece of tarmac.

His unlikely pitch was located right on the edge of the estate and as popularity of his coaching sessions increased, he heard rumors that Westminster Council were planning to rejuvenate the area. So, he seized his opportunity, asking the Council and estate manager to invest money to create an all-weather AstroTurf pitch with floodlights.

Despite the obvious social economic benefits of this project, including but not limited to physical and mental well-being and breaking the cycle of gang recruitment, his plea fell on deaf ears.

"They turned me down and said that residents would never agree to floodlights because they were so intrusive."

Ahmed insisted that he would put it to residents himself and call a community meeting. He said, "I told them that if they agreed to my proposal, crime would fall because instead of youngsters hanging around stairwells, and harassing residents and smoking and drinking, they would be so tired from football that they would go straight home for dinner. I said we would teach the youngsters how to behave decently as well as football skills."

The meeting happened, he stated his case, and there were knowing nods and sounds of approval—but you never really know what the outcome will be until you receive the message.

"The next day I got a message from the residents' association to go ahead—and that instead of the 7pm floodlight curfew I had asked for, the lights could stay on until 9pm."

Without genuine passion for this project, the confidence that Ahmed demonstrated when standing his ground with the local authorities simply would not have been possible. It marked a crucial point in the fight against crime on the estate, and it was the birth of an incredible charity called London Tigers.

Today, the Lisson Green Estate has a state-of-the-art pitch, floodlights, and adjoining facilities. Not only do the football coaching sessions still operate but they also have expanded into seven further estates across several boroughs, now helping 800 children at any given time.

In addition to this, London Tigers operates a semi-professional football club and a cricket club in the county cricket league and is itself an award-winning charity. Mesba Ahmed has personally been awarded the prestigious MBE award (Member of the Order of the British Empire) for his services to his community.

Did this incredible endeavor start with just a desire to make a better life for his children, or was there a passion for football within him?

When Ahmed reflects and relives his glory moment from his short-lived, semi-professional career as a 17-year-old footballer, his love of the game is apparent: "I went past two defenders, just left them for dead, and then I scored an incredible goal that my former teammates still talk about ... I had the potential and it was my dream to be a professional footballer but for people on our estate there was little chance."

This is what drives him. This is his passion and, without this as his guide, he wouldn't have the tenacity to continually challenge the status quo.

He has said, "I suppose it's my secret ambition to discover the first Asian David Beckham. We have never had an Asian play football for England. Mostly what I focus on, what I try to do, is provide a fun outlet for young people away from gangs. At the end of the day, it is about giving youngsters on these estates the opportunities that people like me never had." Ahmed channeled his passion for football to create a thriving charity that has benefited countless children, providing them with opportunities they would have otherwise lacked. And he's not done yet.

As Chief Executive Officer of London Tigers, he continues to evolve the organization. As well as introducing disadvantaged youths to grassroots sports, London Tigers introduces young adults to the joys of coaching. It places hundreds of potential coaches onto official courses and then distributes them across 15 London Boroughs. The ranks of the newly qualified coaching team include individuals who had experienced homelessness, asylum seekers, refugees, and former gang members. And having just signed the lease on a fabulous new sports ground, they are going to need additional coaches.

Sometimes a desire to help, or to affect change is not always enough, especially when you continue to butt heads with the local community and government who don't seem to realize the difference that your vision could have. The emotionally charged connection that you have with your legacy, will guarantee that you have enough gas in the tank to keep going when others try to hold you back.

Create your legacy based on your passion. Ask yourself the following questions:

- What am I passionate about?

- What was the moment in my life where I felt most alive?
- How can I focus my legacy on this feeling and my passion?

The emotionally charged connection that you have with your legacy, will guarantee that you have enough gas in the tank to keep going when others try to hold you back.

Ultimately, if you can pursue your passion with purpose, no one will be able to stop you. Eventually, just like Ahmed, the world will recognize the value in helping you achieve your vision.

Our legacy is made over a lifetime, but it can be influenced by a single moment. And we can create a legacy through a consistent series of moments. We recognize that most people cannot dedicate 100 percent of their life to a legacy project. By re-blending our lives, we can find a little time in each week to place one of the building blocks of our legacy on such a regular basis that eventually our legacy is fulfilled.

Our legacy is made over a lifetime, but it can be influenced by a single moment.

We discuss life blending in more detail later in the book.

CHAPTER 13

PRINCIPLE 3: BE GUIDED BY YOUR PASSION – CHILDREN ARE NOT YOUR ONLY LEGACY

Part of your legacy is your "why" beyond your children. Parenthood is the driving force that compels many people to make a difference in the world, shaped by personal experiences, values, and ambitions. While many people define their legacy primarily through their offspring, it is crucial to recognize that your impact can, and should, extend further. For those who do not have children, the concept of legacy still holds significant meaning. This chapter is for everyone, regardless of parental status.

Take, for instance, the story of Sir Richard Branson, the renowned entrepreneur and founder of the Virgin Group. Branson's legacy is encapsulated in his business empire and the lessons and values he imparts to his children. In a conversation with Ivan, Branson emphasized the importance of living a life of purpose and adventure, encouraging his children to pursue their passions and make a difference in the world. This approach highlights a crucial aspect of legacy: while our children are an integral part of it, our influence should inspire them to create their own paths and legacies.

Often, our children become part of our "unplanned legacy," one that is built through subconscious moments and fleeting actions. And, when reflecting on our own relationships, we come to realize that our parents impact us in ways we don't know until later in life.

One of our authors recounts:

"Whatever work ethic I have, I got from my father. He was a blue-collar laborer who held down a full-time job and one or two part-time jobs for most of my childhood. At the same time, he always found time to spend with the family.

"When I was a young boy, I remember him coming home one weekend evening from his second job and I asked him if he would go outside and play catch with me. My mom said – 'let your father sit and relax a while. He's been working almost 60 hours a week for the last several weeks.' However, my dad said to my mother, 'he's only young once, he needs this time with me,' he then turned to me and said he'd 'love to play catch.' I had no idea at the time, how tired he was and yet how important he felt that it was for him to spend time with his son. The balance between his work ethic and his paternal ethic was something I learned to truly admire as I grew up.

"Whatever people skills I have, I got from my mother. She was very outgoing and people oriented. She could strike up a conversation with anyone, anywhere, at any time. She also had more health problems than anyone I've ever known (heart attacks starting in her 30s, pre-diabetic, knee problems, weight issues, insomnia, cancer surgeries, and to top it off, she was hit by a hit and run drunk driver and lost her right arm). And yet… she was the happiest person I've ever known.

"I once asked her how she could be so happy most all of the time and she said to me that 'the secret to happiness in life is to learn how to change. And then change again. Then change again. Then change again. If we don't learn how to cope with change, we will never be happy' she said. 'She was so right.'"

We recognize that that the influence that our parents have on us is massive, and we also recognize, that for some, years are spent undoing the "unplanned legacy" bestowed upon us by them. To ensure that his is always a positive influence, Branson often uses the analogy of circles to describe the layers of influence and impact we can have. The innermost circle represents our immediate family and loved ones, but as we move outward, our circle of influence can encompass our community, our industry, and even the world. This perspective encourages us to think broadly about our legacy and how our actions can ripple outwards to create a lasting impact.

Your "why" is deeply rooted in your past experiences, shaping who you are today and guiding how you wish to change the world. By reflecting on our past, we can better understand the values and lessons that have influenced us and use this understanding to inform our actions in the present. This reflective process is crucial for building an authentic and impactful legacy.

> **Your "why" is deeply rooted in your past experiences, shaping who you are today and guiding how you wish to change the world.**

In the present, we are actively working on our legacy. Each decision, action, and interaction contributes to the legacy we leave behind. It is an ongoing process that requires conscious effort and alignment with our values and goals.

Parents often reflect on what they want for their children. Their primary wish is for them to be safe, happy, and secure. This desire is shared by most parents, forming a fundamental part of their motivation. However, parents should also recognize that legacy should extend beyond their children.

Consider these three stories of individuals and how their personal legacy fits in with family life.

Nicholas Winton, a British stockbroker, created an enduring legacy through his extraordinary humanitarian efforts during World War II. In 1939, he organized the rescue of 669 Jewish children from Nazi-occupied Czechoslovakia, bringing them to safety in Britain. His efforts, initially kept secret even from his family, were only revealed decades later when his wife discovered a scrapbook detailing the children's rescue. Winton's legacy is defined by his selfless actions and the lives he saved, many of whom went on to achieve significant accomplishments in their own right. His story is a testament to how one person's actions can create a lasting impact beyond their immediate family.

Hudson Taylor, a British missionary to China, not only had children who carried forward his mission work but also established a legacy that significantly influenced global missionary practices. After enduring personal tragedies, including the loss of children and his wife, Taylor continued his work with unwavering dedication. He founded the China Inland Mission (CIM), which was revolutionary in its approach to cultural integration and indigenous leadership. Taylor's legacy lies in his innovative missionary strategies and the profound impact his organization had on spreading Christianity in China, which continues to this day through the significant growth of the Christian community in the country.

Eglantyne Jebb, the founder of Save the Children, created a global legacy that extends far beyond her lifetime. After witnessing the devastating effects of World War I on children, she dedicated her life to advocating for their rights and welfare. In 1919, she established Save the Children, which has since grown into a worldwide organization providing aid and support to millions of children in need. Jebb's work not only impacted her immediate environment but also set the foundation for ongoing humanitarian efforts globally, demonstrating how a singular vision can lead to enduring change.

These stories illustrate how individuals can create lasting legacies through their contributions to society, humanitarian efforts, and innovative practices, impacting countless lives and future generations.

While many people find their primary motivation in their love for their children, it is important to realize that our legacy can be much more far-reaching. Stopping at the idea of children being the sole legacy is limiting. Our children, wonderful as they are, will create their own legacies, influenced by but independent of us. Our legacy can encompass our contributions to our community, our professional achievements, the values we promote, and the changes we drive in the world.

> **Stopping at the idea of children being the sole legacy is limiting. Our children, wonderful as they are, will create their own legacies, influenced by but independent of us.**

Many people see their children as their Infinite Legacy, a continuation of their values and aspirations through successive generations. While this is a significant and noble aspect of legacy, it is essential to recognize that our potential impact is much broader. By considering our influence on a wider scale and striving to make a difference in various spheres of life, we can create a legacy that is truly lasting and transformative.

In essence, crafting a meaningful legacy involves looking beyond the immediate and considering how our actions today can shape a better future for all. It is about understanding our "why," reflecting on our past, and actively working towards a legacy that extends far beyond our children, touching lives and inspiring change for generations to come.

CHAPTER 14

PRINCIPLE 4: CONNECT WITH YOUR COMMUNITY – START LOCALLY, GROW GLOBALLY

As dusk falls on the Friday evening of a holiday weekend in mid-August, a team of workers descend on a now deserted racecourse in the heart of Surrey, United Kingdom. A day of racing, betting, and celebrating has finished, and it is the job of this crew to get the racecourse ready for a very special event.

Working tirelessly through the night, placing banners, signs, flags, pennants, and the traditional finishing line horseshoe, this is the only event in the annual calendar where all other sponsorships and endorsements are covered by a single logo, a single, big red heart.

Because tomorrow is the Variety Club race day, a very special event that sees hundreds of underprivileged children treated to a day at the races. While they are there, they are fed, entertained, and shown—even just for a day—that life can be joyous and full of laughter and fun. This wholesome event was started by individuals with a much smaller vision. Let us explain…

Imagine finding yourself in the age-old cliché of discovering an abandoned baby, crying in a lonely location, with nothing but the clothes they are wearing, the basket they are in, and a single note pinned to their dress. This sounds like the beginning to a film, one where we follow the life of the orphan as they go on to overcome adversity and achieve greater and greater things. However, this story, is more about the 11 men that discovered this child, and how their selfless act went from simply helping one, to impacting millions of children across the globe.

Formed in October 1927, in Pittsburgh, Pennsylvania, "The Variety Club" was a group of 11 close friends, who wanted to formalize their fellowship. They decided on the name due to their background in the performing arts. Members had experience in film, theatre, circus performance and even the ice capades, so "Variety" seemed very apt.

At the Sheridan Square Movie Theatre, on December 24, 1928, (yes, Christmas Eve, as if this story couldn't be more emotionally charged), this group was enjoying a ritual hand or two of cards, following an afternoon performance, when they heard a noise coming from the, now empty, auditorium.

As the men traced the source of the faint whimpering, they were greeted with the sight of a tiny newborn, only a month old, placed on a cinema seat, with the said note attached to her dress.

"Please take care of my baby. Her name is Catherine. I can no longer take care of her. I have eight others. I have always heard of the generosity of people in show business, and I pray to God that you will look after her."

Signed "a heartbroken mother."

Upon the discovery, calls were made to local authorities and press in a desperate attempt to find the parents of this small child. When the minutes, hours, and days, began to tick by, with no contact from Catherine's parents, The Variety Club came to the realization that the immediate wellbeing and the future welfare of this life, lay solely with them.

A decision was made that they would act as godfathers, tasked in equal parts with overseeing her initial upbringing, education, and, of course, her happiness.

Upon taking legal responsibility for the child, they named her Catherine Variety Sheridan.

Keeping her first name as written on the note, with her middle reflecting on her 11 Godfathers and in tribute to their amazing act, and her surname, after the movie theatre where she was found following the matinee performance.

It really does sound like the beginning to an award-winning narrative, and so compelling was this story of 11 selfless men adopting a tiny, abandoned baby, that it quickly came to the attention of the local, then national press across America.

It was the spark that ignited people's flames.

Members of their own industry offered help and assistance to underprivileged children in their local area. So inspired were they by this story, they wanted to establish their own fellowships and emulate the incredible act of protecting the most innocent and vulnerable in the community, children.

In addition to people asking how they could help, physical donations flooded in. Everything imaginable that would be needed on the journey from infancy through childhood began to turn up.

The only problem was there was simply too much for baby Catherine alone, so the Variety Club started bundling clothing, toys, and books, and found other children and families in need to donate to.

Fast forward almost 100 years and this charity has now donated over half a billion dollars to children in need, across the globe. This organization has grown naturally, through the established network of actors, singers, and performers, and never loses site of where it came from, 11 men, brought together by a common love of the performing arts.

You can see this respect permeating through every level of the Variety Club. When a new location opens, it is named after the Circus Big Top and is called a "Tent." Variety Club members are called "Barkers," the title of the man at a carnival or circus who would "bark" to gain the attention of the crowds.

When you do the right things for the right reasons, the world takes notice. These 11 men made the choice to make a difference to Catherine, a single human life. Because of this, their community, their network, and the world, took notice and the Variety Club now operates in 14 countries and will shortly celebrate its centenary.

If you start locally and use the network you have in front of you, your legacy has the potential to grow globally.

If you start locally and use the network you have in front of you, your legacy has the potential to grow globally.

One of our authors, Ivan, found himself in a similar situation to the members of the Variety Club. His story, too, is one of starting locally— "one man, in one town." This quickly developed into a global movement, now impacting hundreds of thousands of people annually.

What follows is the interpretation of his fellow authors, having interviewed Ivan about the legacy and impact he has had during his lifetime as founder of BNI$_®$, and the BNI Foundation.

(As with the origin story of BNI in our previous book, *Infinite Giving*, it certainly wasn't going to be Ivan who wrote this chapter.)

It seems natural to start with BNI because it came first, and it began as his quest to find a better way of doing business. Ivan had gone to many different networking groups, but they did not resonate with him. Some were very mercenary in the way they operated, and he felt like he needed a shower after being sold to so much. Others were totally social, and no business was being discussed at the meetings. What he wanted was something that had a focus on business but wasn't mercenary while being relational but not totally social. Not being able to find one, he started a group for himself as well as his friends and associates. His group quickly began to gain popularity and notoriety, spreading out of its original town, across state, over the country, and into international territory. BNI has impacted millions of business owners over the last four decades, and now annually contributes billions of US dollars into communities around the globe.

There are members that not only credit their ongoing business success to BNI, but also cite it as a life-changing organization, allowing personal development, mentorship, and much needed support, when often there is nowhere else to turn. Ivan himself is humbled when he sees the impact that it has had on so many people, one that has exceeded his wildest expectations.

In every sense of the word, BNI is a legacy. So, we posed the question to Ivan, "when did you first realize that BNI had become *the* legacy that you would leave to the world?"

He shared that it was the moment that now happens every year at BNI's Global Convention—one that marks the grand opening of this multinational, multicultural multilingual event: the flag ceremony.

This is where a representative of every nation that has an active BNI chapter, walks in holding their country's flag. Organized from longest established to newest global family member, BNI now encompasses almost 80 sovereign states, with many of their bearers in traditional dress.

Prior to the first ceremony, in the late 1990s, the flags of the United States, Canada, United Kingdom, Australia, and Ireland, would simply appear on a banner behind the speakers. With a rapidly expanding international community, the spectacle of this inaugural event with dozens of countries waving their flags, represented the moment that Ivan realized that BNI would become an important part of his legacy.

He said, *"that was the point in my life where it really sunk in that we were changing the way the world did business."*

Our work with Ivan has shown us that he is truly a strong believer that your life is your legacy. It's not just what you achieved, but how you live your life, how you show up in it. We could have highlighted multiple aspects in Ivan's life that will act as a legacy. He has produced an incredible body of work from best-selling publications to extensive blogs, and a podcast library with a consistency and longevity of which is rarely seen. He also has a property portfolio, a beautiful art collection, a wine cellar which many aspire to popping a cork in, and of course, his family.

That your life is your legacy.

He also considers his interactions with others as a lasting legacy, which, of course, can be good and bad. We, his co-authors, have personally witnessed Ivan's small acts of kindness and been told stories from many others.

He tells the story of two directors popping their heads around his office door to say hi, and upon seeing them, Ivan stopped his work, and invited them in for a drink. The normal humility of interrupting anyone followed: "We only wanted to say hi," "We didn't want to bother you."

Ivan responded with *"This work will be here tomorrow, you won't."*

"This work will be here tomorrow, you won't."

This moment of genuine warmth and hospitality has now been retold by the Director in question on multiple stages in multiple countries and is now being recounted in this book.

These interactions don't even need to be in person; they can be electronic via email phone call or, in this case, social media. Recognizing that a fellow BNIer was having a rough time after reading a Facebook post, Ivan commented with something along the lines of "You've got this, you're really good, you're doing great."

Ivan can't remember exactly what he said. However, the recipient of this small act of kindness can because they framed a printed screenshot on their office wall, in full view of anyone who they have an online meeting with.

We recognize that the intangible things like how you make people feel or being the curator of an art collection or the owner of a historic building, means that legacy can also include how you leave the world in terms of your interactions and not only your creations.

With no set retirement date in mind, and no need for financial support from BNI, Ivan considers BNI less as a vocation and more as an avocation, not like a hobby but like a calling. He loves pouring himself into his calling and seeing the difference it makes. He has the full intention of standing on stage at a global convention, celebrating 50 years of BNI in 2035.

There aren't many who would bet against Ivan being on that stage. His fellow two authors wholeheartedly agree with a compliment that he received: *"He's like an older fast ball pitcher, but instead of losing his edge, he's throwing faster today than he did when he started out."*

BNI is still his passion. It is still where he finds himself. He is working in his flame (doing what he loves) and not in his wax (doing things that don't bring him joy). Most importantly, he still wants to throw that fast ball.

Seeing BNI continuing to grow, in the coming decades, Ivan envisages representation from every entrepreneurial nation in the world, becoming a household name, with millions of members, creating a ripple effect of trillions, that would place BNI in the top 10 of GDP nations. If it were considered a country of its own, as of today, there are currently 100 countries in the world with a LOWER GDP than what BNI generates in business for its members.

While no legacy is ever protected, Ivan is good with who he is, how he shows up in the world, and how positively how he has impacted the people he has met. Always striving to do what's right for its members and the communities around them, he realizes that some legacies have been built on fear and intimidation. BNI has been built on positivity and support, meaning it has the very best of chances to perpetuate on and on for centuries.

Why then, with the impact that BNI has across borders, religious and political boundaries, was there the need for the BNI Foundation? Ivan attributed the nonprofit he co-founded with his late wife, Elisabeth Misner, to their desire to take the good that BNI does a step further.

Elisabeth and Ivan used to contribute to great causes, mainly with a focus on children and education. Finding that their overflowing cup was increasing also meant their giving activities could increase. They both decided that they didn't just want to give money each year, so instead they created a foundation, where they could sustainably contribute to wonderful causes over time.

Ivan and Elisabeth both held a strong belief that they should give back to the communities which they draw from.

For a number of reasons, they felt a moral and ethical obligation to support education and children, because, as Elisabeth often said, *"Children represent 20 percent of our population, but they are 100 percent of our future."*

> **"Children represent 20 percent of our population, but they are 100 percent of our future."**

Starting with only $10,000, the BNI Foundation has now given almost $10 million to charitable causes around the world. In addition, the BNI Foundation's endowment now stands at almost $1 million.

In a perfect example of Infinite Legacy, the BNI Foundation has now created Business Voices, a business team that can move quickly where local BNI members and community leaders are personally giving back their time and expertise to projects such as painting a classroom, educating the next generation of entrepreneurs, or turning wasteland into a community garden, allowing us to point to a physical manifestation of the ripple effect.

To find out more about creating a ripple in your local community, please visit www.bnifoundation.org.

For most people, reading Ivan's story might feel intimidating. But like so many legacies, Ivan's launch of BNI started small. He focused on his immediate locality— "one man, in one town." He has repeatedly stated:

You may not be able to make a world of difference, but you can make a difference in the world.

> **You may not be able to make a world of difference, but you can make a difference in the world.**

Those are words we should all remember. Your legacy is a multi-faceted contribution to the world. It's not just about giving money, and it's not just about giving time. It is a combination of all things.

The world is a little more positive, a little more supportive, and a lot brighter because people like this are part of it.

When the line is drawn under Ivan's life, and the deeds are summed up, there will be countless people who have felt the impact of his time with us.

Having said that, two out of three of the authors of this book still believe his fastest pitches are yet to come.

CHAPTER 15
PRINCIPLE 5: ACT WITH URGENCY – WRITE YOUR OBITUARY

So here it is—the chapter you were expecting from the moment you picked up this book. Most personal and professional development books will, *in some form*, pose the following type of question:

"How will you be regarded when you're gone?"

> **"How will you be regarded when you're gone?"**

In fact, one of the go-to publications when people embark on their journey of self-development, *The Seven Habits of Highly Effective People* by Dr. Stephen Covey, asks you to imagine a journey to your own funeral.

Told is the story of jumping into your car, driving to a place of remembrance, taking in the sights of the flowers, the sounds of the light organ music and sitting down on a pew, looking at an order of service, only to realize that you are at your own funeral.

Within this order of service are listed four speakers:

1. A family member
2. A close personal friend
3. Someone from your professional life
4. Someone from your community

Dr. Covey continues to ask, "What would you like them to say?"

It's a fascinating exercise. We highly recommend everyone undertake it during their review and goal-setting time, as it can help focus one's mind on what's really important. However, one of the most poignant things about this exercise is that Dr. Covey limits this scenario to three years! Yes, you'll be attending your funeral in just 36 months.

Depending on your stage of life and your current health while reading this book, 36 months may seem like an incredibly short period of time or an amount that you are longing for. So, in the tradition of all good personal development books, this is the moment where we remind you that life is so much more than an endpoint. It's about the journey we close for ourselves.

While writing this book, it became apparent to us that no one leaves this world with a completed to-do list. There will always be movies unseen, music unheard, places unvisited, relationships unamended, and goals unachieved.

While writing this book, it became apparent to us that no one leaves this world with a completed to-do list.

This is why it's vitally important to include legacy in your planning. Legacy has the potential to continue to grow without your input, so when the moment of departure comes, your obituary will read in the way you would like it to.

So, what will your obituary say? If this is the first time you've been asked that question, it may be overwhelming, and often people respond with outstanding acts.

- Topping the rich list
- Winning an Oscar
- Curing a disease
- Saving a nation

But for most of us, the small acts, the incremental gifts that we have left over from the course of our lives, will be reflected in the pages of our orders of services.

Let us help you to avoid the overwhelm. Sometimes, we forget the wisdom of those who have come before us, those people who are a few steps ahead of us on life's journey. They have made the mistakes, learned the lessons, and, more importantly, are willing to share their findings so that we can avoid the pitfalls that they had to overcome.

Dr. Anthony Campolo, an American sociologist, author, public speaker, and former spiritual advisor to United States President Bill Clinton surveyed 50 people over the age of 95 and asked them one simple question:

"What would you do differently if you were allowed to live life over again?"

"What would you do differently if you were allowed to live life over again?"

As you can imagine, there were many anecdotal tales about the trip that wasn't taken, the fish that got away, and the kiss that never happened. However, three reoccurring themes emerged from the tears and laughter of recounting memories from almost 5,000 years of existence.

1. **<u>Reflect more.</u>**

    Take time to stop, look around, and pay attention to what you currently have in your life. Use the time to show gratitude and plan your next step.

    Life shouldn't just be the meaningless passage of time.

2. **<u>Risk more.</u>**

    The majority of the 95-year-olds in the survey didn't examine their lives in terms of success and failure but rather by the risks that they either took or, in most cases, didn't.

    Some might word this as simple regret. However, setting yourself a goal of regretting less is intangible, whereas setting yourself the target of embracing risk seems more achievable.

    One of the authors of this book, when reflecting on their life thus far, simply says, "Every success I've had in life has come from me throwing my hat in the ring."

    Whether we realize it or not, we all take risks. Dr. Campolo pointedly stated "You can't have friends without risk, you can't engage in a marriage or relationship without risk, and you can't have a fulfilling career or purpose without risk."

Unless you're reading this in your bedroom, having had no social contact for many years, we have all "put ourselves out there" at some point.

As a side note, if the sentence above describes you, take the opportunity, the risk, to reach out to one of the authors and tell us what this book has meant to you. Who knows where that risk may lead?

3. **<u>Do more things that will live on after you're dead.</u>**

    Wow, okay so we've used the D word. Ultimately that's what your legacy is about—things that will live on after you've died. Of course, we can say "when you're gone," "leave this world," "are no longer here," or many other euphemistic terms.

    But we prefer dead.

    There is something finite about it. There is no mincing of words. Using that word crystallizes our view on what we have to achieve while we have the opportunity. And let's be candid; living is an opportunity that is taken from so many, far too soon.

    Campolo shared, "One of these days, you are going to die. When you were born, you cried, but everyone else was happy. Now when you die, is everyone else going to cry?" If we want to create a lasting legacy, we must do things that matter.

This is where building an Infinite Legacy will have an impact on your own fulfilment and leave a gift to the world around you.

As a reminder, your legacy doesn't have to be huge. You don't have to put your name on the side of buildings, you don't have to win awards, cure illness, or champion social mobility. (However, you can, of course, do all of those things if you'd like and if you can.)

Your legacy may be small. It might be a trinket, or a document left as a gift to future generations, a charity, or a social enterprise that refreshes and impacts the community around you, or that "one good book" that everyone is said to have inside them.

When thinking about your own obituary, imagine first that you didn't make Stephen Covey's 36-month deadline. Perhaps your deadline was 24, 12, or even just 6 months away.

What do you have in front of you right now? What opportunities present themselves on a daily basis, and what small risks could you take to begin to build your own Infinite Legacy? What small tasks or actions can you do that benefit others that also align with your passion and purpose in life?

Do this for each of the four previously mentioned areas: family, friends, profession, and community.

While this may seem slightly macabre, it is, in fact, incredibly liberating. It is like crossing two or three small tasks off your daily to-do list. It gives you a sense of achievement and the motivation to continue, knowing actions we can take right now can make people smile in years to come.

If you're still struggling, have you written down the recipe for your "go-to" meal, perfect cake, or signature cocktail? There are things we wish our loved ones had passed down to us; it would be a simple and immediate step for you to ensure yours don't feel the same.

However, one of our authors is quite happy that their nan's slow-cooked grey cabbage delicacy has been lost to the mists of time.

He much prefers her tip of collecting seeds from flower heads, keeping and drying them in an envelope, and sprinkling them between the cracks of a patio when spring comes. (Thanks for the flowers, Nan xoxo.)

There are things we can impact today that will make a difference tomorrow if we take time to reflect and react.

There are things we can impact today that will make a difference tomorrow if we take time to reflect and react.

Once you've looked at the immediate, start looking at the mid-term, and take the three-year time scale. What can you build on given the foundation that you've listed above? What can be a continuation of the legacies that came from the immediate opportunities, and what are the new gifts that we can begin to grow in that period, given proper planning?

Finally, we can look at our long-term legacies, the culmination of our life's work and dedication, which take years and decades to form, not just days and weeks.

This reflection and action-oriented exercise prepares you to write your obituary. And, yes, we are serious that you should take time to write it. Write multiple versions. By taking the time to write an immediate, mid-term, and ultimate obituary that includes all four areas of our lives, you begin to form a road map for our journey of existence and legacy. You can think about how you want to influence your family, friends, profession, and community. Writing your obituary may seem like a morbid task, but it can be a valuable exercise in reflecting on your life and legacy.

> **By taking the time to write an immediate, mid-term, and ultimate obituary that includes all four areas of our lives, you begin to form a road map for our journey of existence and legacy.**

Additionally, writing your obituary can help you to plan for the future and to ensure that your loved ones are prepared when the time comes. It can direct your actions for today and tomorrow because one of the critical things to consider when writing your obituary is how you would like to be remembered. Think about the most important things to you and the values you hold dear. Consider the impact that you have had on the world and the people around you. Reflect on your accomplishments, the things you are proud of, and the lessons you have learned. By thinking about how you would like to be remembered, you can gain a deeper understanding of your values and priorities and use this information to guide your actions in the present.

It's also important to note that writing your obituary can also be a powerful exercise in gratitude. It can help you appreciate the time you have and make the most of it. It can also help you focus on the things that are truly important in life and prioritize the things that matter most to you.

By taking the time to think about how you would like to be remembered and what you want to leave behind, you can gain a deeper understanding of your values and priorities.

> **By taking the time to think about how you would like to be remembered and what you want to leave behind, you can gain a deeper understanding of your values and priorities.**

In this book, we provide examples of many different legacies, culminating in the experience and research of the three authors and those around them. It will not, however, be a complete list. There will be things that you see, projects that you embark on, and gifts that you impart that will be new, unique, and part of your journey.

We would LOVE to hear about them. At the end of what could be quite a solemn chapter, we hope that writing your own obituary will give you focus and purpose for the entirety of your life.

It is false to say we only live once. We actually only die once. We have the opportunity to live every single day. When you were born, you cried, and people were happy. When you die, people will smile through the tears and be grateful that they knew you.

> **It is false to say we only live once. We actually only die once. We have the opportunity to live every single day.**

CHAPTER 16
PRINCIPLE 5: ACT WITH URGENCY – LIFE BLENDING

One of the limiting beliefs that people have about legacy is that they do not have the time, talent, and treasure that it requires. This belief is false, and the solution to it is in the practice of life blending (also known as work-life harmony).

In our life, we have limited resources and, indeed, limited time. We can, however, be discerning in how we spend our time. Because of this, there are infinite ways we can blend our lives with many people and activities while still taking time for ourselves.

Both Greg and Julian have a keen interest in the joy of drinking whiskey. Whiskey is a blend of flavors created by distillers since the early fifteenth century. The exact origins of whiskey are lost in time. It is widely acknowledged that Scotland is the birthplace of whiskey with the first distilleries established in the seventeenth century.

In August 2018 Julian travelled to Dufftown in Scotland, the home of three world famous distilleries in the heart of Speyside, which is renowned for its whiskey production. The trip involved tours of distilleries and learning the art of whiskey production. If you have never been to that part of the world, then please put it on your bucket list; it is stunning, beautiful, and full of history and heritage.

Blending in whiskey production comes in many forms. You can vary the ingredients, for instance, by adding peat during the kilning of the malt. People hotly debate the merits of a strong peated taste. Distillers use a small amount of peat each time and it totally changes the taste or the blend of the whiskey. Where the water comes from also effects the taste of the whiskey, so much so that William Grant who own two of the Dufftown Distilleries (Glenfiddich and Balvenie) have purchased much of the local farmland that contributes to the water source they use. This way they can lease the land to farmers and be in control of what goes into the soil and water. The shape of the stills contributes to the taste as do the barrels used to store the whiskey and what was previously in those barrels. And to bring together blending and legacy, the length of time whiskey spends in the barrels changes the taste. More on this later.

The number of variables in the production of whiskey is one of the reasons why whiskey lovers like it so much. The variety means there is always new things to discover and a new taste experience in the next bottle.

We know that many of you will not be fond of whiskey. What they say in Scotland is "you just haven't tried enough yet to find the one you like."

Distillers employ highly trained master blenders. One of the most famous employed by William Grant was David Stewart MBE, who was responsible for most of the blends of taste, aroma, and flavor in their products for many years. His job was to create and blend whiskey with complexity and delight for millions to enjoy.

Your job is to blend and re-blend your life so that you can enjoy it for your whole life. As with whiskey, if you are not enjoying your life then you have not yet found the blend(s) that suit you. We say blends because we can create many life blends that we can move between and constantly update them.

> **Your job is to blend and re-blend your life so that you can enjoy it for your whole life.**

For instance, at some point in our lives, we might have to put 80 percent of our waking time into our studies, 10 percent into eating, and 10 percent into family and socializing. Let us consider another extreme example. When caring for a sick spouse or relative, we may need to put 75 percent of our time into caring for them, 10 percent into eating, 5 percent into another family member, and 10 percent into checking in with our workplace.

Generally speaking, life is not as extreme as these examples, and we can choose a more balanced life blend. The primarily consideration when spending your time is self-care. This is because if you are not strong and healthy, you cannot show up for others meaningfully.

Below is a life blending table that is by no means exhaustive and in no particular order of how you might spend your time, and it gives you a good idea of the items you may choose.

Activity	Percentage
Exercise	
Eating	
Income generation	

Activity	Percentage
Legacy project	
Close family time	
Extended family time	
Hobby 1	
Hobby 2	
Housework	
Watching TV	
Playing computer games	
Reading	
Spending time with friends	
A side hustle	
Volunteering	

When you list the things in your life that are important to you, you can decide what percentage of time you want to dedicate to that activity, which becomes your life blend. Life blending is wonderful because you can change it whenever you want, and there is no right or wrong way to life blend, provided your blend positively influences your life and the lives of those you care about.

We can also have multiple blends: one for holidays, one for deadline days, one for spring, one for winter, etc. There is no end to how we can choose to spend our time; the key consideration is to do it on purpose, with strategy and in a positive way to our lives.

Often, society talks about work-life balance. Life blending or a life of "harmony" are, we believe, the superior replacements to work-life balance. The expression work-life balance is the cause of much stress in the world. This is because people are influenced into thinking that spending time on work is bad and that spending time on life is good. Furthermore, it prompts many people to feel that we should be looking to balance these two undefined things perfectly—and if we get it wrong, we are in some way a bad person. Often a negative work-life balance is portrayed as us neglecting our family or ourselves.

Life blending or a life of "harmony" are, we believe, the superior replacements to work-life balance.

The concept of life blending is a superior way of looking at time allocation because it acknowledges three essential things about how we divide our time.

1. There is no right or wrong way to spend our time.
2. We can change how we spend our time depending on current priorities.
3. Sometimes to make room for one area of our lives, it is OK to cut back elsewhere.

Once you consider your priorities, your life-blending list will take shape. For example, your list might look like this:

1. Self-care and staying healthy
2. My primary income
3. Family
4. My secondary income
5. My social life

It's a slightly controversial list. Many people will say their family is their number one priority. Another perspective, however, is that if you neglect your health and income, then you cannot help your family. We share this sample list to give you permission to put something other than family as number one, if you choose. Remember, there are no right or wrong lists.

Where does legacy sit in this priority list? We maintain that you can start to build a legacy at any point in your life and that your life is your legacy. Based on that assumption a legacy project should always be considered as part of your life blend. We will not say that you must have it in your blend. Otherwise, that would risk us falling foul of "there is no right or wrong way to spend our time." What we are saying is always to consider legacy when you re-blend. Does it make the cut? Can you find a percentage or two of your time to create your Infinite Legacy?

Like many things in life, the best time to start was 10 years ago, and the next best time is now. If you feel you have not yet begun to leave a legacy, you can be confident that if you choose to, then now is a great time to start. Maybe watch slightly less TV or wake up slightly earlier. If you decide to make room for legacy in your life blend, we know you will be rewarded when you start seeing the results.

If you feel you have not yet begun to leave a legacy, you can be confident that if you choose to, then now is a great time to start.

Interestingly, the distillers in Dufftown understand all too well about legacy. William Grant is a family business which can trace its story back through generations starting in 1887. In its warehouses are barrels of whiskey dating back many years. Some of the whiskey made today in the distillery will never be sold by the current family members. It will be sold by future generations just as the current custodians of the business have sold whiskey made by previous generations. This is legacy in action.

CHAPTER 17

PRINCIPLE 5: ACT WITH URGENCY – CREATING A LEGACY WITH BELIEF, PASSION, AND LEADERSHIP

When all is said and done, our life is our legacy. We believe Sartre got it right when he said that your deeds are your life; so, the question is, how do we build a foundation of deeds that will help us leave a strong legacy?

The three characteristics in this chapter are important in creating a legacy that lives on past your lifetime. In many ways it requires a reset of one's mindset or a pivoting from where you are to where you want to go with your legacy.

Belief

First, you must believe. You must believe that you can pivot your life and/or your business or career and find ways to help more people and create an Infinite Legacy. You must believe in what you can do for people.

You must believe that you can pivot your life and/or your business or career and find ways to help more people and create an Infinite Legacy.

There is an old story of two shoe salesmen who were sent to different parts of a developing nation to see if there was a market for their shoes. After a week, the first salesman wrote back to the company and stated, "No one wears shoes here. There is no market for us. Send me a return ticket." The second shoe salesman, in the same country and under the same circumstances, wrote back to the company and said, "No one wears shoes here. There's a huge market for our shoes. Send me a large shipment."

You must believe in yourself and the people around you. That means you need to consciously pivot your belief system in what is possible, so you can achieve the legacy you want. When faced with challenges, people who believe they can pivot do so successfully and all of the people who believe they cannot pivot fail. Like Henry Ford has commonly been attributed to stating, "Whether you think you can or you think you can't, you're right."

Pivoting to create a legacy always begins with the belief that you can.

Passion

Next you must have passion about what you do and how you will achieve it. But let us be clear about passion. Passion does not produce commitment. Commitment produces passion. Commitment and passion produce results. It is the CPR for your life

(C+P=R). Nothing great in life has ever been done without passion and commitment.

> **Passion does not produce commitment. Commitment produces passion. Commitment and passion produce results.**

Leadership

The third key is leadership. Leadership is not about managing and complying; it's about mobilizing and inspiring. Over the years we've learned that Theodore Roosevelt's words ring true that "people don't care how much you know until they know how much you care." It's about the touch points you have with the people in your life.

> **Leadership is not about managing and complying; it's about mobilizing and inspiring.**

- It's about connecting with people. It's about giving the people in our life love, care, and attention.
- It is about inspiring people to take action.
- It's about guiding people and helping people. Day in and day out—it's about showing up to help them be a better version of themselves. That's what leadership is.

Don't over complicate things! We don't know why people make things so complicated, but we do. Things don't have to be complicated. Making progress toward a positive legacy is about:

- Belief
- Passion
- Leadership

We've seen ordinary people do extraordinary things. Anyone can do extraordinary things with the right belief, passion, and leadership. We believe that our vision controls our perception, and our perception becomes our reality. Set a vision that makes a difference to the people around you.

We've seen ordinary people do extraordinary things. Anyone can do extraordinary things with the right belief, passion, and leadership.

It's all about vision and moving toward that vision no matter the obstacles or challenges that get in your way. There's a reason why your windshield's larger than your rearview mirror. It's important to have the clearest view possible of where you are headed. As a result, your windshield is substantially larger than your mirrors. Of course, it's important to know what's behind you and to learn from where you've been. However, if all you are looking at is your rearview mirror, it's because you're going backwards. When you do that in life, you are not living in the present and you are not aware of what may be ahead of you.

If all you are looking at is your rearview mirror, it's because you're going backwards.

Sometimes in life we do need to go backwards a little way. However, as soon as possible, we need to put that car in Drive and move on to our intended destination. To get to that destination, we should have a map or an app to take us where we intend to go. Sometimes, we must take an alternate route because of heavy traffic or accidents along the way (both good metaphors for life). But in either case, you need to have a general idea of where you want to go.

We know people who work really hard and are always very busy, but they don't set life or career goals. Most of these people are lost. They are lost because if you don't know where you want to end up, going faster won't get you there quicker.

Windshield wipers are another great metaphor for life. Sometimes the weather is so bad that you need something to help keep things clear. Other times, you need even more help than that.

Ivan recalls a time he was driving with his family up to their lake house in Big Bear, California. Suddenly, they hit a patch of fog that was so incredibly thick, he could not see the road in front of him! Worse yet, they were driving up a mountain so he couldn't see any place that was safe to move off the road. So, he rolled down the window and stuck his head out and literally drove ahead looking down at the little white ceramic Botts Dots that are on so many highways throughout the country. (By the way, they are called Botts Dots after Elbert Botts who invented them in the 1950s.)

He drove very, very slowly staying in alignment with the Dots while his wife looked ahead to warn him if she saw the lights of any oncoming cars. After a mile or two, the fog cleared enough for him to roll up his window and simply drive ahead slowly.

The metaphor for this is that sometimes we may need an assist to get where we are going. The key is—we generally need to continue to move forward (safely of course) in order to get to where we want to go.

Don't let objects obstruct your view out of your windshield. There will be people in life that will get in the way of where you are heading. Don't let them. Keep the windshield of your life as uncluttered as you should keep the windshield of your car.

Don't let objects obstruct your view out of your windshield. There will be people in life that will get in the way of where you are heading. Don't let them. Keep the windshield of your life as uncluttered as you should keep the windshield of your car.

Your rearview mirror is to see what is behind you. From this moment forward, know that it is the view out that windshield that will take you where you want to go in life. To leave a lasting legacy, it is essential to look forward and not backwards.

Stewart Emery, author of *Built to Last*, shared a story with Ivan over breakfast one morning, recalling an interview he did with a well-known billionaire in the computer industry.

The billionaire shared an intriguing moment of an experience he'd had when the senior executives of a rival firm in purchasing his company visited his office to discuss the possible purchase.

At lunch, the billionaire told the senior executives of the company he was negotiating with that he was going to take them to the Executive Dining Room.

They followed him to the dining room which was very nice but not extravagant. But that wasn't the big surprise. The surprise was that the dining room had a buffet line. Moreover, the billionaire walked up to the buffet line, picked up a tray, and stood in line behind everyone else.

The executives looked around the room as it filled up and they realized that this room was not an "executive dining room" but was the company dining room. The boss stood there in line with all the employees. He spoke to everyone. No one was afraid to talk to him. He didn't lead by being above them; he led by being among them.

The management team was surprised by the fact that he and all the executives ate with all the employees. One of them commented that "this would have to change."

For the boss, it was a test. This was not the kind of company that he wanted to sell his business to. The negotiation ended that day.

He led that company with a strong belief of its identity, one that he had helped establish. He had the passion, leadership abilities, and vision, to turn away a potentially lucrative deal because he knew and understood the path they were on.

Sometimes when people meet Ivan, they say that they are surprised that he is approachable. People feel this way because leaders often act in a way that people perceive as unapproachable. They act "better than" other people. We believe people should be surprised when a leader is unapproachable, not when they are approachable. The problem is that we live in a world where success sometimes creates a sense of separation between the high-achieving person and everybody else.

However your legacy may grow, there is a strong chance—given time, consistency, and persistence—that you will find yourself in a position of leadership.

Taking action, while maintaining your vision, and acting with passion and belief will ensure that those who are already along for the ride will remain with you, and, just as importantly, the new people who join you on your journey will be of the right mindset to help achieve your Infinite Legacy.

For those who believe in "The Law of Attraction," always remember that the word "action" is part of the word attraction. We must take action to achieve the legacy we want to leave behind.

Today more than ever we need to ask ourselves, why accept mediocrity, when excellence is an option? And excellence is always an option. Even during difficult times, we must always strive for excellence.

Today more than ever we need to ask ourselves, why accept mediocrity, when excellence is an option?

CHAPTER 18
PRINCIPLE 5: ACT WITH URGENCY – YOUR LEGACY IS NEVER SECURE

We've come to the chapter where we hold a mirror up to the fragility of legacy and highlight how something that people can spend a lifetime creating can in fact, be torn down in a matter of days, or in extreme cases, seconds.

Whether it be a lifetime of evil, dichotomous behavior from an entertainer coming to light, the final proof of systematic and sustained cheating to achieve sporting greatness being brought to public attention, or a recorded act of madness following a traffic stop leading to a drunken tirade of anti-Semitic rhetoric, a personal reputation and, more importantly, the good of a created legacy attached, can be destroyed in an instant.

The building of a legacy, therefore, should neither be a confessional penance to offset other sins, as we are sure some are, nor should it ever be assumed that what we have built cannot be torn down by our actions, both past and present. For two of our authors, it has again been a privilege and an honor to work alongside Ivan Misner PhD, noted by CNN as the father of modern networking, someone who, founded BNI, the world's largest networking organization.

Considering this organization at time of writing (2024) has more than 328,000 members and growing, is represented in over 75 countries on six continents, it was said with an almost flippant confidence during an exploratory conversation about this book that, "Ivan's legacy was secure" by one of his co-authors. Ivan refuted the claim, stating "a legacy is never secure." His point was clear; any one of us could invalidate our legacy.

Ralph Waldo Emerson was quoted as saying "Life is a journey, not a destination" and your legacy is no different. Like all journeys, we must consider the route we're taking, the vehicle we're using, the passengers that we allow to share the road with us, and, most importantly, who is in the driver's seat.

"Life is a journey, not a destination" and your legacy is no different.

Above all, we must consider the journey we're on. Is it right for us to take this journey?

Are we creating the legacy because we genuinely want to leave the planet in a better state than we found it or are we trying in some naive way to transactionally offset some of our behavioral deficits from the past? It's a strong question and one that we should ask ourselves.

If we refer to the opening story in this book, we may naively assume that a right outweighs a wrong. Afterall, Alfred Nobel erased the negative connotations around his name after learning his reputation while reading his own obituary. He went on to build an impressive Infinite Legacy.

We would be incorrect in this assumption.

For Nobel, although his invention had been used in the most heinous of ways, it was always his intention to save lives using his abilities as a chemist and it was only when his discovery was applied in warfare, without his permission, did his name become synonymous with death. The creation of the Nobel Prizes, the committee that judged and the lasting trust that would fund the ongoing furtherment of humanity, was more in line with Nobel's core values. Nobel's negative public perception at the time of the accidental obituary was already known and turned out to be a fallacy, so the building of a positive legacy in line with his true beliefs enabled a lasting memory to be built in a fashion that he had always intended.

Imagine if, in an alternate universe, the Nobel Prize had been established, Alfred had been celebrated during his lifetime, and then, only after his demise, had it come to light that he had secretly been designing weapons of mass destruction and selling them on the black market to those that would use them against innocent women and children. The now celebrated annual awards would have had to have been renamed, rebranded, repurposed, or removed altogether.

The above is what we have seen happen to many legacies once hidden scandals and behaviors were discovered.

Our best advice to ensure the security and longevity of your legacy then is to build one in line with your core values and beliefs and to continue living to those standards for as long as you are lucky enough to do so.

If Dr. Evil happens to be reading this book, no number of playgrounds for orphaned children, shelters for homeless veterans, or freshly bored wells for thirsty families will ever offset the secret lairs in hollowed out volcanos, lasers on sharks' heads, or trapdoors into lava pits.

Our advice to you then, would be to give all of your money anonymously to a legacy that is already secure with no expectation of recognition or reward. This may allow you then, at the very least, one good night's sleep.

We can say that legacy is never secure. But we are also certain that if it is built on a foundation of passion and belief in line with a strong set of core values and backed by your moral code, it will only be an act of self-sabotage or temporary insanity that will stop it from becoming a true Infinite Legacy.

CHAPTER 19

PRINCIPLE 6: THINK LIKE A STONEMASON – POSTHUMOUS LEGACY

Ok, wow. This was a tough chapter to write. The concept of committing wholeheartedly to a belief or a concept during your lifetime only to have your efforts go unrecognized during your mortal existence seems painful. But over and over again, amazing examples of legacies only ever taking hold posthumously can be referenced.

We must mention these posthumous legacies to give credence to the work and struggle of many who came before us. Our lives today and the lives of many generations to come have been enriched by the foundation of those who never got to experience the benefit or recognition of their labor.

This reminds one of our authors of an early story that he posted on his Twitter account. Luckily, we can use more than the 140 characters that he was limited to at the time.

A nobleman walked the construction site of his recently commissioned cathedral. Barely above the foundation stage, the current course of masonry stood at about waist height. The final plans called for flying buttresses and a towering spire, which ultimately would take generations to complete. While inspecting the site, the noblemen came upon two stonemasons, both working on similar-sized pieces to slot into this giant jigsaw. Upon approaching the masons, he noticed a stark difference in their expressions. Approaching the first of the masons, he was greeted with a formality that nobility dictated and then went about asking a question.

"Tell me what it is you're doing."

"My Lord, I am chiseling this stone to square it off; when it's the right size, it will be marked and put into place along with countless others by the master mason. Eventually, we will complete another course, and when enough masons complete enough stones to make enough courses, we will have finished the project. This won't be in my lifetime, nor will it be in the lifetime of my children or my children's children; it's backbreaking work and of which, I will never see the final result, but the pay is good, and I can support my family."

Our nobleman noticed that while his work was quick and efficient, it was vacant. There was no joy and no purpose in his actions, and this was clearly reflected in his general demeanor.

"Tell me what it is you're doing."

Moving on, our nobleman approached a much more animated, vibrant, and lively mason and, after formalities were done repeated the question.

"Tell me what it is you're doing."

"My lord, I am building a cathedral."

"My lord, I am building a cathedral."

The original tweet is below if you're wondering how that was ever condensed down into 140 characters.

"1st stone mason complains that it's backbreaking work & won't be completed in his life. 2nd smiles- "I'm building a cathedral" #thestoryfella"

Yeah, it kind of works, kind of.

We've included that story because the people who leave posthumous legacies, like the second stone mason, must have believed that what they were doing would ultimately build something amazing.

There are many examples of posthumous legacies from every facet of society.

In science, Alfred Wegener, who in his lifetime was known mainly for his achievements in meteorology and as a pioneering researcher of the polar regions, is now most remembered for his hypothesis on continental drift, on which all modern geological theories are based. His hypothesis was widely rejected and hugely controversial in the early twentieth century. It wasn't until the 1950s that discoveries in areas such as paleomagnetism provided strong support for continental drift, leading to the model of plate tectonics we accept today.

Gregor Johann Mendel, now referred to as the father of modern genetics, didn't receive recognition for his ground-breaking work in his humble monastery garden. Upon his death in 1884, the scientific community negated and ignored his work. It wasn't until three decades later that the scientific community accepted and revered his experiments of crossbreeding pea plants of various colors. Gregor noted that when you bred a plant with predominantly yellow foliage and a plant with mainly green the resulting offspring would always be a yellow plant. Gregor theorized that something in the yellow plant pushed out the green element and took dominance in the offspring. We now understand and refer to the yellow aspect of the plant as the dominant gene and the green coloration as a recessive gene. When Gregor's work was rediscovered, it ushered in the modern age of genetics.

In literature, Stieg Larsson proves that this "overlooked genius" phenomenon is not a thing of the past. He was the author of the Millennium Trilogy, the most famous of which is *The Girl with the Dragon Tattoo*. These books were only published posthumously after their author's sudden death from a heart attack in 2005. His books have sold 100 million copies worldwide and have been made into three motion pictures in Sweden, one of which, *The Girl with the Dragon Tattoo*, was made for the international market. Daniel Craig played the lead role. Publishers have even commissioned David Lagercrantz to extend the original three to six books. Stieg Larsson's original trilogy is recognized as one of the very best in crime fiction.

There are so many examples of people who never got to experience the true impact of their work.

In music, we could speak about musicians such as Nick Drake or Jeff Buckley. In cinema, even though they experienced fame during their lifetime, the legacies of film stars such as James Dean and Bruce Lee were never truly established until after their demise.

The most famous of these posthumous legacies has to be that of artist Vincent van Gogh. Irrespective of your background or how you have pronounced his surname while reading this (officially, the Dutch say Hoh, like you're breathing out, with both g's silent, but the debate rages on), his name resonates in the minds of everyone who hears it. Whether it be images of the night sky, sunflowers, or a strangely haunting self-portrait, the majority of us would recognize one of his works if presented with it.

In his life, Vincent van Gogh only sold a single painting. He sold it for, in today's money, just over $110. Today his portfolio of more than 2,000 works offers an unrivalled artistic legacy, with each piece priced in the millions of dollars.

The story of his life is as tragic as his paintings are beautiful. We could, as many have, dedicate an entire book to his life and works. Commonly many people know the story of him cutting off his own ear, and it has been widely accepted that he battled with bipolar disorder throughout his short life. It would be easy to view this simply as a tragic tale, with even the gun used to shoot himself at the age of 37, rediscovered in 1965 and auctioned in 2019, described as the "most famous weapon in art history" being sold for more than $180,000, seen as a final insult to his story. We would much rather consider the joy, inspiration, and serenity that his pieces offer the world, something that he famously strove for in his own life and never obtained, but now ironically, provides to millions.

In 2010, on the flagship BBC sci-fi show *Doctor Who*, writer Richard Curtis righted a universal wrong, at least in fiction. The episode sees the doctor and his companion travelling back to nineteenth-century France to battle an invisible monster manifested in one of van Gogh's paintings, The Church at Auvers. The culmination and highlight of the episode come when van Gogh travels forward through time to his own exhibit at the

Musée d'Orsay. Visibly stunned by the displays, he becomes emotionally overwhelmed when hearing the curator say van Gogh was the greatest painter of them all and one of the greatest men who had ever lived. The episode was a love note from Richard Curtis, screenwriter *of Four Weddings and a Funeral, Love Actually*, and the Bridget Jones series, to an artist who had never received admiration or respect for his work but continues to inspire people today.

Whether we believe that the above-mentioned geniuses understood that their work would one day gain notoriety, we must believe that they believed in their work and purpose.

Time and again, it has been shown that once a legacy has been correctly established, it will continue to grow long after the departure of those who laid the foundation.

> **Time and again, it has been shown that once a legacy has been correctly established, it will continue to grow long after the departure of those who laid the foundation.**

Always be the second mason. Understand that you're building a cathedral.

CHAPTER 20

PRINCIPLE 7: HAVE AN INFINITE MINDSET – PERSONAL LEADERSHIP TO LEGACY LEADERSHIP

Don't let people come to your funeral guessing what your legacy is.
—John C. Maxwell

Throughout this book, we have emphasized that your life is your legacy, a powerful concept that empowers you to start shaping your legacy from the moment you are born. Your legacy is not something that waits for a particular moment to begin. It starts whether you are aware of it or not. While many people may be oblivious or indifferent to the legacy they are creating, the truth is, we are all creating something, whether we realize it or not. It is far more fulfilling and impactful to develop one's legacy with consciousness and purpose, a journey that can inspire and motivate you.

Given that our life is our legacy, the choices we make each day, no matter how small, will inevitably contribute to our ultimate life legacy. We hope to inspire more individuals to begin creating a conscious legacy from the earliest stages of their lives, and to use the perspective of legacy to guide their daily decisions.

> **While many people may be oblivious or indifferent to the legacy they are creating, the truth is, we are all creating something, whether we realize it or not.**

To make better decisions each day, we need to study and master personal leadership. Personal leadership is about taking charge of your own life and responsibilities, a journey that holds immense potential for personal growth and capacity expansion. Part of growing as a person is to always be ready to expand your capacities and strengths. Many people in life do not see themselves as leaders. This is a falsehood. Regardless of the hand we have been dealt with in life, we all can be a personal leader and take charge of our actions and decisions. Personal leadership is the building block that all great leaders have. Without personal leadership, our broader leadership can be very erratic. This realization should fill you with hope and optimism about your potential for growth and leadership.

> **We hope to inspire more individuals to begin creating a conscious legacy from the earliest stages of their lives, and to use the perspective of legacy to guide their daily decisions.**

Personal leadership is also linked with discipline and consistency. We need discipline and consistency to deliver many legacies. We must focus on achieving our goals and work relentlessly toward them.

Personal leadership is the building block that all great leaders have.

A compelling illustration of personal leadership in action is the journey of David Beckham, the globally recognized soccer player turned businessman. It's easy to assume that individuals like Beckham are inherently talented, that they were born with a specific skill, in his case, soccer. But the truth is, skills are not innate. They are not a product of nature or nurture. Our skills are shaped by the decisions we make every day.

Beckham was as good as he became because of his work ethic (a legacy from his father). Beckham practiced relentlessly. In his 2013 book titled *David Beckham* he recalled how he worked at taking free kicks repeatedly. "I must have taken tens of thousands" [of free kicks], he said. He would hang tires from the goalposts and repeatedly aim for those posts. He would also go to his local park, place the ball on the ground and aim at the wire meshing over the window of a small community hut. "When my Dad got home from work, we would go over to the goalpost together. He would stand between me and the goal, forcing me to bend the ball around him."

Beckham faced a pivotal moment during the 1998 Soccer World Cup when he was sent off during England's match against Argentina. That red card led to immense scrutiny and criticism. However, Beckham's journey from that low point to becoming a global superstar showcases resilience, determination, and the power of redemption. Let's explore how he transformed his legacy:

During the match against Argentina, Beckham kicked Diego Simeone and received a straight red card. England eventually lost in a penalty shootout.

The aftermath was brutal: effigies of Beckham hung in pubs, and he faced relentless abuse from fans and the media. It was so bad that Beckham revealed that he was clinically depressed after the incident. The abuse took a toll on his mental health, affecting his eating, sleeping, and overall well-being. But David Beckham is made of strong stuff, and he again worked as hard as anyone to make an impression and create his legacy.

By the time Beckham left English football in 2003 to begin a globetrotting adventure, he had won six Premier League titles in eight seasons and was a central figure each time. He led the Premier League in assists on three separate occasions and was selected in four PFA Teams of the Year.

As England's captain, Beckham's performance in an iconic game against Greece in 2001 is a perfect summary of Beckham the footballer. It wasn't just that he scored the crucial free-kick to secure his country's place at the World Cup; he was the best player on the pitch that day long before he stood over the dead ball, dragging his team with him throughout, fighting for every inch and never giving up.

Beckham worked hard on and off the field. He became a global ambassador for soccer and, in the United States, for Major League Soccer (MLS). His MSL legacy lies in elevating MLS and inspiring future players.

People often did not give Beckham enough credit for this side of him, especially as his celebrity status grew as the 1990s became the

2000s. Today, his legacy in England and around the world is huge, both within soccer and outside of it.

In the end, David Beckham's journey from adversity to triumph exemplifies the power of resilience, reinvention, and the ability to turn negative moments into positive legacies. All of that started with a little boy practicing free kicks in the local park with dedication and consistency.

The most decorated gymnast of all time, Simone Biles, has exemplified personal leadership as well. Despite immense pressure, Biles withdrew from most events in the 2020 Tokyo Olympics after experiencing the "twisties," a condition in which gymnasts lose spatial orientation in aerial moves. Her actions spurred intense criticism and shone a spotlight on mental health issues. Biles, however, returned to the Olympics, and in 2024 won four medals at the age of 27. (And did we mention she was the oldest United States gymnast to compete in the Olympics since the 1950s?) Biles stayed true to herself and is blazing a legacy that is sure to become infinite.

It is never too late to start taking control of our personal leadership and making decisions that will one day lead to us creating the legacy we want to give to the world.

It is never too late to start taking control of our personal leadership and making decisions that will one day lead to us creating the legacy we want to give to the world.

Personal leadership is just the start; it's an enabler for us to go on to great things. We can deliver our dreams when we choose to act with purpose. Ultimately, we can become outstanding leaders in our lifetime. Pinnacle Leaders are defined in John C. Maxwell's excellent book *The 5 Levels of Leadership*. In the book, Maxwell describes Pinnacle or Level 5 leaders as those who create a legacy in what they do. There is more to being a legacy leader than creating a legacy. People operating at this level can create an environment that allows others to create their legacy and lead in a way that creates new leaders. This then makes an organization that perpetuates its mission.

Legacy leadership is the pinnacle of creating your legacy through leadership. Our journeys start with personal leadership. Many of us will never get to legacy leadership. However, knowing that is a path some people can follow, we can study and learn to get the most out of our legacy projects.

The Walt Disney Company offers a tale of both personal and legacy leadership. In the early 1920s, a young artist named Walt Disney embarked on a journey fueled by imagination and determination. Alongside his brother Roy O. Disney, Walt founded a small animation studio in a garage. Little did they know that this humble beginning would evolve into a global entertainment empire.

Walt Disney was more than an animator; he was a dreamer. His vision extended beyond cartoons. He believed in creating a magical world where families could escape reality and experience wonder. With the creation of Mickey Mouse in 1928, Walt set the stage for what would become a cultural phenomenon.

Walt was both a creative genius and a demanding taskmaster. His relentless pursuit of perfection drove his team to achieve the impossible. He pushed boundaries, introducing synchronized sound in animation with "Steamboat Willie" and later revolutionizing the industry with the first full-length animated feature, *Snow White and the Seven Dwarfs*.

Walt left an indelible legacy that continues to shape the world of entertainment, creativity, and dreams. His impact was multi-faceted. Walt Disney was a trailblazer in the American animation industry. His innovations transformed the production of cartoons, introducing techniques that captivated audiences worldwide.

As a film producer, he achieved unparalleled success. Walt Disney holds the record for the most Academy Awards earned and nominations by an individual. His contributions were celebrated with two Golden Globe Special Achievement Awards and an Emmy Award.

These accolades recognized his exceptional creativity, storytelling, and dedication to pushing artistic boundaries. His legacy extends beyond entertainment. He founded the California Institute of the Arts (CalArts), a school dedicated to training future artists and storytellers. Graduates of CalArts, including luminaries like John Lasseter and Tim Burton, have become some of today's leading filmmakers and have created their legacies.

Walt Disney embodied optimism. His belief in the wonders of the world inspired his creative endeavors. The song "Feed the Birds" from Mary Poppins encapsulates his personal view of life—a simple act of kindness can make a profound difference.

Walt's vision extended beyond animation. He conceptualized EPCOT (Experimental Prototype Community of Tomorrow), a utopian city of innovation and progress. Disneyland, the first-ever theme park, opened in 1955. It became a testament to his imagination and a place where dreams come alive.

Even in his 60s, Walt maintained a hectic work pace. Retirement was not in his vocabulary.

His commitment to storytelling, innovation, and goodness drove his relentless pursuit of new ideas and ambitions. And so, Walt's legacy lives on—a beacon of creativity, kindness, and boundless imagination. His impact reverberates through every frame of animation, every theme park attraction, and every heart touched by the magic he conjured.

When Walt's creativity soared, Roy's feet remained firmly planted on the ground. As the financial backbone of the company, Roy ensured stability during turbulent times.

After Walt's untimely death in 1966, Roy took charge. His pragmatic leadership guided the completion of Disneyland and the ambitious Disney World project in Florida. His leadership ensured that the Magic Kingdom was constructed to Walt's specifications and that Disney maintained operational control of the resorts. Roy's dedication to his brother's legacy was unwavering. Roy played a pivotal role in the development and success of Disney theme parks. He was instrumental in ensuring that Disney retained control of operations at Disneyland, setting a standard for the immersive experiences that Disney parks are known for today.

Roy was key in fulfilling another of Walt's dreams: the establishment of CalArts. Under his supervision, CalArts broke ground for its current campus, nurturing future generations of artists and storytellers. Roy O. Disney's legacy is not only in the financial stability he brought to the company but also in the enduring values of dedication, foresight, and responsible stewardship that continue to guide The Walt Disney Company today.

Others have continued the Disney legacy. Donn Tatum was CEO of the company from 1966 until 1971. Donn Tatum stepped in as interim CEO after Roy's passing. His tenure was brief but marked by continuity. He was the first non-Disney family member to lead the company, guiding it through a period of significant growth and expansion. He played a major role in creating Walt Disney World Resort, EPCOT Center, and Tokyo Disneyland. In recognition of his contributions, Tatum was named a Disney Legend in 1993.

The Disney Legends program is a Hall of Fame award established by The Walt Disney Company in 1987. It honors individuals who have made a significant impact on the Disney legacy. The program recognizes gifted animators, Imagineers, songwriters, actors, and business leaders whose contributions have significantly shaped the company's history and culture. The Disney Legends award symbolizes the appreciation for the remarkable talents and achievements of its recipients. It includes three distinct elements:

The Spiral: Represents imagination, the power of an idea.

The Hand: Symbolizes the gifts of skill, discipline, and craftsmanship.

The Wand and the Star: Denotes the magic that occurs when imagination and skill combine to create a new dream.

The program relates to legacy leadership as it celebrates the enduring contributions of individuals who have upheld and advanced the values, vision, and creative spirit of The Walt Disney Company.

By acknowledging these influential figures, the Disney Legends program ensures that their legacies continue to inspire current and future leaders within the company. It serves as a reminder of the importance of leadership in fostering a culture of innovation, storytelling, and excellence that defines Disney.

The Legends are chosen by a selection committee, which was formerly appointed and chaired by the late Roy E. Disney. This connection to the Disney family further emphasizes the program's role in preserving the company's heritage and guiding its ongoing leadership philosophy.

The next person in our legacy leadership chain at Disney is Card Walker who was CEO between 1971 and 1983. Esmond Cardon "Card" Walker was instrumental in maintaining the company's direction and momentum during the transition period after the death of the Disney brothers. He was CEO when the EPCOT Center and Tokyo Disneyland opened. These projects were significant in establishing Disney as a global entertainment brand. Walker founded the Disney Channel in 1982, contributing to the diversification of Disney's media offerings and its entry into the cable television market. He successfully navigated the company through uncertain times while preserving Disney tradition and expanding its magic around the globe.

In recognition of his contributions, Walker was inducted into the Disney Legends in 1993, celebrating his impact on the company's history and culture. His legacy is one of leadership, foresight, and commitment to the enduring values and vision of Disney.

Michael Eisner was the Disney CEO from 1984 until 2005 when his arrival signaled a renaissance. He revitalized animation with films like *The Little Mermaid*, *Beauty and the Beast*, and *The Lion King*, restoring the studio's reputation for classic animation. Eisner's tenure saw the creation of Disney's Animal Kingdom, a groundbreaking theme park that combined thrilling attractions with zoological habitats.

Eisner's financial acumen led to impressive stock price growth and increased company valuation. From four parks to 11, from 2,500 hotel rooms to 32,000, Eisner led a huge growth period for Disney parks.

Bob Iger CEO from 2005 until 2020 led the acquisition era for Disney; he acquired Pixar, Marvel, Lucasfilm, and 21st Century Fox. Disney's global footprint expanded, and Shanghai Disney Resort opened. Iger's boldest move was launching Disney+, a streaming service that disrupted the industry. His leadership emphasized storytelling and innovation.

Iger's legacy extends beyond Disney's borders. His leadership made Disney a global entertainment powerhouse (increased revenue from $2.5 billion to $10.4 billion), touching millions of lives through storytelling, theme parks, and media. Iger had an unwavering commitment to the magic of Disney and its traditions. Iger returned to his leadership role in 2022 after Bob Chapek's termination, signaling that Disney's Board of Directors want him to continue to shape Disney's legacy for years to come.

As each CEO left their imprint, Walt and Roy's spirit endured. The parks, films, and characters continue to enchant audiences worldwide. The personal leadership that evolved into legacy leadership at The Walt Disney Company is a testament to resilience, creativity, and the belief that dreams can come true.

Personal leadership is a fundamental aspect of effective leadership. Personal Leadership sets the tone for how we interact with others. If we can't lead ourselves, it's unlikely we'll lead others effectively.

By mastering personal leadership, we create a solid foundation for guiding and inspiring those around us. Personal leadership allows us to develop a clear vision for our lives. When we understand who we are, what we value, and where we're headed, we can pursue our goals passionately and purposefully.

> **Personal leadership allows us to develop a clear vision for our lives.**

Effective personal leadership involves self-awareness. Knowing our strengths, weaknesses, biases, and motivations helps us make informed decisions. Cultivating a growth mindset allows us to learn from setbacks and continuously improve.

Leading oneself also means building resilience. When faced with challenges, we bounce back, learn, and adapt. Resilient leaders inspire confidence and create a positive work environment.

By understanding ourselves, we can better understand and connect with others. Authentic self-leadership fosters trust, respect, and collaboration within teams and organizations.

As John C. Maxwell astutely stated, *"Everything rises and falls on leadership."* In summary, personal leadership is a prerequisite for effective leadership that positively impacts individuals and those in our network. When applied to our legacy projects, this foundation supports our legacy, long after we are there to guide it.

> **"Everything rises and falls on leadership."**

CHAPTER 21

PRINCIPLE 7:
HAVE AN INFINITE MINDSET –
WRITING YOUR MEMOIRS

Writing your memoirs is another legacy-building activity that fosters personal reflection and growth, creative expression, and inspiration for family and descendants. This type of writing can at first seem like a daunting undertaking. For some of us, especially in our most self-deprecating moments, it can feel self-centered and a little egocentric.

Our internal monologue begins asking questions.

Who am I writing this for? And would anyone actually want to read it?

Then, those questions are often followed by statements like…

My life really hasn't been that interesting… Is it even worth documenting?

The truth about memoirs is that they can be, and can offer, a multitude of services. These range from the cathartic to the educational, and can be written for all to see, or simply a select few. Perhaps your memoirs will offer a private and deeply personal account that will only ever be read by your closest family and friends. Or could they be an education piece to help transfer wisdom and knowledge acquired during your lifetime to those that follow? They can also help others by being a biography of the journey that you've been on, one where you have overcome adversity, struggle, and strife, and act as inspiration to those who are two, three, four, or five steps behind you on the same or similar journey. And of course, they can be a historical record of a time and life, which no longer exists, one that you want future generations to be aware of.

If you choose to write a memoir, don't worry about writing best seller. This activity is typically more for your family and yourself than any public audience.

Memoirs can fall into one of four different categories, the descriptions of which are summarized below.

1. Confessional – Consider this a therapy session on a page, something that you know you've wanted to write down, an itch that needs to be scratched. This is normally the family secret, only known to a few, that unfortunately seems to come out only upon the passing of the holder, but when shared, becomes the light bulb moment that clarifies to others exactly why and who you are.

The confessional could be a burning issue, a dark secret, some hidden trauma that has never been officially shared, the unseen key that would help others close to you, to unlock your true self. And for this type of memoir, its often easier to write these events and allow others to read, than it ever would be to share face to face. However, the feeling of absolution when transferring to paper can be as uplifting as sharing at a group therapy session.

2. Teaching – This is a compendium of knowledge and skills, systems and processes, and wisdom and insight collected through a lifetime of learning and education.

What makes this different to a standard "how to" manual is the personal inflection that you add alongside the instructional text. Say, for example, you have spent your lifetime creating jams and preserves from hedgerow fruits, found on countryside rambles. A cookbook would simply tell you to add a certain weight of fruit along with a certain proportion of sugar, and then list additional steps to complete the process. Any of us who have tried to follow a recipe knows the difference between textbook learning and real-life execution.

Now imagine you were reading the memoirs of someone who had spent time understanding the very best moment to pick fruit so that the flavors permeated perfectly into the final product. They were able to convey the nuances of steaming jars to increase the shelf life and would even be willing to share the mistakes that they had made during their almost limitless attempts, so that you could avoid the temptation and distraction of going down the same path.

This is where teaching memoirs add incredible value. They also offer us an insight to the author as their personality shines through the words on the page. We, as readers, carry the author with us as we begin on the same journey that they, too, started many years before.

3. Transformative – Have you had that moment when you look at your current life, then you find yourself thinking back to where you were five, ten, or twenty years ago? You may even be transported to your childhood, reliving some of the events, both good and bad.

The question that tends to follow a moment of reflection such as that is "How did I get here?"

Whether we realize it or not, there must have been a moment or a period/process of transformation because we would not be asking ourselves that question if our lives now looked exactly as they did when we were children.

We could have escaped or overcome poverty, social boundaries, educational restraint, religious expectations, parental shortcomings, sexual or gender stereotypes, abuse, addiction, or simply self-imposed limiting beliefs. Whatever your watershed moment, or moments were, there will be people that are looking for some assurance and guidance who follow you on the same path.

Your memoirs will become their "it's gonna be okay" moment.

4. Historical – These can be a deeply personal but factually accurate, depiction of a very specific person, place, organization, or moment in history.

Take trench art, for example, not officially part of the World War I arts program, but a much sought after antiquity prized by collectors. When the guns were silent, and during moments when soldiers were not on duty, skilled young men used discarded shell casings to create incredible pieces of art. These outpourings of creative talent offer an insight into trench life, very different to the officially commissioned oil paintings and bronze statues that are on display in public locations today.

Historic memoirs offer a similar insight. They could be the day-to-day life of a resident living in a village, town, or city, recalling the characters, the personalities, the moments of joy and diversely those of sadness experienced by them and their neighbors, which vary drastically from the records and official photographs of the town planning documents.

It could be the view from the terraces of an avid fan of a sports team, walking through packed streets, dressed in club colors, and singing fan created songs, offering a very different account to league stats and player interviews.

Or the memoir might be a retelling of a harrowing journey of exodus from a once safe homeland, across continents, oceans, and borders, to find sanctuary as a refugee following the outbreak of war. These personal stories cut through to the hearts and souls of the readers, more than any official stats about troops moved, bombs dropped, or lives lost.

Our editor, Heidi Giusto, previously worked on a project involving a soldier's journal from the American Civil War. The soldier's descendants desperately wanted to read his account of the Civil War but were unable to read his handwriting. Their solution was to have it professionally transcribed. After, they were able to read not only about the battles he was in but also about the frequent hunger soldiers experienced and the issue of desertions. The journal breathed life into a historical event that feels distant to his descendants, taught them about a member of their family, and is a treasured family heirloom. What a service the soldier did for his family!

Historical memoirs really do add depth and personality to often two-dimensional official records.

An incredible example of how a memoir can encompass many of the above is that of Jeanette Winterson (author of *Oranges Are Not the Only Fruit*). She writes about a life dedicated to finding happiness.

Winterson recounts stories of being deliberately locked out of her house in Lancashire, England by her religious zealot mother and having to spend the whole night sitting on a cold stone step. When discussing this moment of abuse, Winterson's humor brings a smile to the reader's face. She gleefully tells us of chugging the bottle of milk that was meant for her mothers' morning tea. She left the empty bottle on the step, ready for her mother to find it. Then, Winterson skipped off to school, safe in the knowledge that she had had "the last word" in that argument, even if it was a fleeting victory.

Her semi-autobiographical novel, set in an English Pentecostal community, touches on many of the "struggle" points we listed previously and would have certainly inspired others on the same or similar journey to keep going. Her work is confessional, transformational, historical, and educational, and continues to be as relevant today as it was when published in 1985.

We can all work on our memoirs—it is a legacy piece that is open and accessible to all.

There are no rules when writing memoirs, but the truly great ones are where the authors are open, honest, and authentic. They share their most intimate experiences without hesitation and build trust, they make us laugh, they make us cry, but above all else, they are a true reflection of the writer and the world around them during their journey.

We have incredible tools to hand to help us begin writing our memoirs: audio and video recorders in the palms of our hands; easily accessible, storable, sharable, and editable electronic documents; and the opportunity to capture high resolution images, without the need for delayed and costly developing.

Even if you are writing your memoirs primarily as a family heirloom—something to pass on to your relatives, a record of who you are, and to forever become part of your family's social history—you may find that others become interested in your story and it grows into part of your Infinite Legacy.

One of our authors has memoirs from his mother and grandfather. They are fascinating reading, and he wishes he had more memoirs from other family members. Who in your life wishes they had your story to read?

There is no set time to start a memoir. We all are creating our history, week by week, month by month, year by year. Is it time to write about those important events in your life?

If you're ready to take this step, we encourage you to get started now. And if you need help, let technology offer assistance. Consider using professional memoir-creating services like Storyworth, which prompts a person to answer a question every week and then creates a book from quality materials designed to last for generations. Other well-known sites like Shutterfly, allow users to create picture books with captions, while many apps can incorporate a combination of written, audio, and visual files. There are books like those produced by Skyhorse Publishing like "Mom's Journal" and "Dad's Journal" that ask many prompts about your favorite memories and activities. This is a great way to share elements of your life that your children and grandchildren may not have been aware of. There are countless ways to document your memoir, helping you to create your own Infinite Legacy.

CHAPTER 22

PRINCIPLE 7:
HAVE AN INFINITE MINDSET – LEGACY IS ABOUT THE FUTURE

Legacy is often defined as something left behind by someone who has passed away or something that is transferred or received from the past. It is an integral part of human history, culture, and civilization. Every individual or group of people, whether they are leaders, artists, writers, scientists, or activists, have a unique legacy that has contributed to the world we live in today.

Legacy is not just about leaving behind material possessions or assets; it is also about the impact that an individual or group has on the world. For example, Martin Luther King Jr. left behind a legacy of civil rights activism that continues to inspire people around the world. His message of equality, justice, and non-violence has resonated with generations, and his speeches and writings have become a part of American history. Similarly, Nelson Mandela's legacy of anti-apartheid activism has inspired people all over the world to fight for justice and equality.

Legacy is also important in the world of art and literature. Artists such as Pablo Picasso, Vincent van Gogh, and Leonardo da Vinci have left behind a rich legacy of artwork that continues to inspire people today. Their paintings, sculptures, and drawings have become a part of our cultural heritage, and they have influenced countless artists throughout history. Similarly, writers like William Shakespeare, Jane Austen, and Charles Dickens have left behind a legacy of literature that has shaped our understanding of the world and human nature.

But you should know by now that legacy is not limited to famous people or historical figures. Every individual has the potential to leave behind a legacy, no matter how small or insignificant it may seem. For example, a teacher who inspires a student to pursue their dreams can leave behind a legacy of education and empowerment. A parent who instills values of kindness and compassion in their children can leave behind a legacy of love and generosity.

The importance of legacy is evident in the way it inspires and motivates future generations. It provides a sense of continuity and a connection from the present to the past it can give people a sense of belonging and identity to something greater than themselves. Legacy can also inspire individuals to strive for greatness and make a positive impact on future generations. However, it's important to recognize that legacy is not solely defined by individual achievements, but also by the societal and cultural contexts in which those achievements occurred.

> **True legacy is not in the success of our endeavors, but in the impact that we have made on others.**

True legacy is not in the success of our endeavors, but in the impact that we have made on others. To leave a lasting legacy, it is essential to look forward and not backwards. Our windshield is larger than our review mirror for a reason. It's important to recognize what is behind us, but what is most important is what lies ahead of us.

Our windshield is larger than our review mirror for a reason.

When we look backward, we become trapped in our past successes and failures. We may be proud of what we have accomplished, but some people may also be haunted by the mistakes that they have made. We may be tempted to rest on our laurels and feel that we have already made our mark on the world. However, this kind of thinking can be misleading, as it can prevent us from moving forward and making even greater contributions.

Instead, we should focus on the present and the future. We should think about what we can do to make a positive impact on others right now and in the years to come. This means investing our time and resources in projects and initiatives that have the potential to change people's lives for the better. We should seek out opportunities to mentor and inspire others, to give back to our communities, and to contribute to causes that we are passionate about. We all have people who are in our story—people who have changed our lives but the most important thing in leaving a legacy in the world is— whose story are we in? Whose life have we changed for the better?

When we take this approach, we can be confident that our legacy will be one of positive change and impact. We will be remembered not only for what we have accomplished, but also for the lives we touched and the people we inspired. We will be remembered as leaders, visionaries, and advocates for change.

Of course, looking forward does not mean that we should forget about the past entirely. We can learn valuable lessons from our experiences, both good and bad, and use those lessons to guide our future actions. But we should not allow our past to define us or limit our potential. Instead, we should use it as a springboard to even greater achievements.

- Our true legacy is not just about the success of our business or what we have accomplished, but the impact we have made on others.
- To leave a lasting legacy, it's essential to focus on the present and the future, and not get trapped in the past.
- We should invest our time and resources in projects and initiatives that have the potential to make a positive impact on people's lives.
- We should seek out opportunities to mentor, inspire, give back, and contribute to causes we are passionate about.
- We can learn from our past experiences and use them as a guide to achieve even greater things.
- Legacy is about inspiring others and making the world a better place.

Legacy is not just about what we have done, but what we will do in the future.

Legacy is not just about what we have done, but what we will do in the future. We should look forward with optimism and a commitment to making a positive impact on the world. By doing so, we can leave a lasting legacy that inspires others and makes the world a better place. Legacy is about creating a life of significance. It is most certainly not about the wealth you leave behind; it is about the impact that you leave behind.

Legacy is about creating a life of significance.

SECTION THREE

CHAPTER 23
PERSONAL LEGACIES

In Chapter 14 we asked one of our authors, Ivan, about his personal legacy. We discovered how it started out of the necessity of finding a better way of doing business but quickly grew into a global phenomenon that has impacted millions either directly or indirectly. With its continued evolution, and the addition of charitable iterations, it is (almost) certain to become a true Infinite Legacy.

Ivan also made us aware of the other many aspects of his life that would be viewed as wonderful legacies if the spotlight were on them alone. He reminded us that we will weave a tapestry, rather than simply spin a yarn, of legacy.

Our two other authors are still working on their legacies, still deciding how they will shape them. Like you are doing now, they are also contemplating what they see as their current and future legacies. We share their thoughts below in an earnest attempt to show that you can still make progress on your legacy project, even if you aren't quite sure what you want it to be. In this sense, you might be building the plane while you're flying it. However, we firmly believe that if you live your life with intent, the day will come when you discover your legacy project. Then, it is only a matter of following Dolly Parton's advice*: "Find out who are you. And do it on purpose."*

"Find out who are you. And do it on purpose."

Julian Lewis

Writing this book has meant that I have considered my legacy and my impact on the world more and more. I have long believed that my children are not my legacy; my personal belief is that this devalues them in some way. Of course, I am part of what shapes the people they are, and I am very proud of them all. They will create their impact on the world, and I hope to see all the beautiful things they achieve.

Legacy for me has always been personal and only started considering once I was in my 50s. I am sure I am not alone. One of the things we want to achieve with this book is to encourage legacy projects to begin at any age. So, I am comfortable that I have started more recently. I also know that the first 50 years of my life will feed into my legacy projects via the knowledge and experience I acquired during those years.

Writing a book is a great place to start creating a legacy. I am very proud of our first book, *Infinite Giving*. It was published during the COVID-19 pandemic and has yet to get as much exposure as it could have. I will continue to promote that book along with this one and the next one. Right now, I am on track to be the author of four books, and writing is infectious; I will not stop there.

In my community, I spent 10 years on the board of my local Rugby Union club. I am very proud of my achievements there, and I did, in my way, contribute to the club surviving challenging financial circumstances. The sport of Rugby Union shaped who I am today. I have friends for life with whom I played rugby in the 1980s and 1990s. I owe a lot to the sport, and I have a desire that it is available to people in my local community forevermore.

I have stepped back from an executive role at the club for now. I am still active in taking a role both locally and regionally, focusing on a critical area for society generally: discipline. When time permits, I intend to step back into the club's executive if they will have me and again play my part in ensuring that the legacy created by the club's founders in 1928 continues forever.

Recently, I was asked, *"If you could live five minutes of your life again, which five minutes would you re-live?"* It is a great question that, for some of us, will expose at least one element of a legacy project we should consider. My answer in the moment was to play five minutes of rugby again. That game would be in my heyday, with those friends who remain the closest of friends to this day. There is power in the fact that I went to that memory instinctively. It is a fact I embrace. What would your answer be to that question, and could it form part of your legacy?

"If you could live five minutes of your life again, which five minutes would you re-live?"

This book applies to me as much as it does to you. I am considering some more legacy projects. Through my involvement in BNI, I have developed a skill in public speaking. I learned this skill through practice and study from a very low baseline. I am not a natural public speaker, but I am proof that it is a skill that can be learned. I want to pay it forward, and as well as talking about our books, I want to work with others so that they can be better speakers. With just a small amount of support, they can share their ideas with a broader audience in a more impactful way. I am working with others on what that will look like. I want to work to make that a legacy project. This is my example of one of the things this book has inspired me to do.

I want to leave my mark on the world, and I hope you do, too.

Greg Davies

Perhaps it's uncommon, but I've never really considered my children to be my legacy.

I have two incredible daughters who are right at the beginning of their adult journey. Abi is an apprentice engineer at the second largest airport in the United Kingdom and Jess, having collected rocks and crystals since she has been able to walk, will be pursuing further studies in geology.

They are two incredible humans, clever, kind, well rounded, and I feel an overwhelming sense of pride while writing this. I had influence (hope there was some good, and I'm sure some unintentionally bad), but, ultimately, they are in control of their own lives. They make their own choices and are masters of their own destiny. I am looking forward to being a spectator when they achieve amazing things.

My primary concern with people who cite their children as their legacy, is at some point, we naturally lose control or influence over the path that they are on. I see many parents who feel lost when their children either leave home or make a life decision that is out of alignment with their own beliefs and views. So rather than our children being our legacy project, I see my role as a parent as more of a teacher, mentor, guide, and friend. But trust me, I don't have all the answers on that one.

So, what is my legacy? What will it be? The truth is, I hadn't seriously considered it until recently, and I'm sure a lot of people who read this book would have been in a similar situation.

I've been lucky to tick off a number of bucket list items in my 45 years, one of which, writing a book, is now one of the strands of my legacy. Knowing that I had to write this passage, however, has made me clarify my thoughts a little further.

September 11, 2001, is the date that so many remember due to the devastating and tragic attacks on New York. At the time I was working on a magazine dedicated to the fire industry in the United Kingdom, and our sister publication, *Fire International*, had firsthand information and unpublished access to the initial response, recovery, and clean up following the attacks.

However, I wasn't in the office when the news broke. My phone was off as I was visiting my late nan (grandmother), in the chapel of rest. She had just passed away, following a battle with a brain tumor. My father and I paid our last respects, jumped in the car and travelled two hours to a private hospital just outside Gatwick airport where my mum had just come around from surgery to remove a third of her bowel, following the discovery of cancer. Indeed, 9/11 was a very painful day.

I remember my mum saying that when she was put under for the surgery, the world was normal and when she woke everything has changed. She was referring to the new global political threat level, and the fact that she now had a colostomy bag as a permanent companion.

During her recovery, her manager came to visit her, and after the flowers were laid on the side, the grapes have been put into a bowl, and the small talk had subsided, he began to ask her fundamental questions about the day-to-day running of his department.

When he saw me looking at him with a quizzical expression, he would joke.

"Your mum secretly runs the place. Nothing gets done without her."

Following conversations in hospital rooms before, during, and after chemotherapy sessions and casual questioning of my father, I now know that my mum was offered promotion multiple times in her life. But her fear of public speaking, writing on the flipchart, and her own self-doubt, made her turn these offers down time and time again.

The more I think about her life—the way she used to draft all our Christmas cards, have my father check for spelling and grammar, and then write them into the final cards—I am a firm believer that she suffered from dyslexia. My mum was brilliant, clever, funny, kind, and she had the ability to elevate those around her. She was an amazing leader, but she didn't have the confidence to take the title.

Whatever final iteration my legacy takes, it will, in some form, give those people who believe they cannot, or have been told they cannot, or should not, every chance to be successful in some important part of their life.

> **Give those people who believe they cannot, or have been told they cannot, or should not, every chance to be successful in some important part of their life.**

I, too, am dyslexic. I struggle to read, and I struggle to write. Yet my journey of self-development was revolutionized when at the same time, I read one book, *The Richest Man in Babylon* by George S. Clason, and listened to another, *Outliers* by Malcolm Gladwell, to test how I absorbed information. I now know I am an audio learner, as I still use some of Gladwell's stories in my presentations more than a decade later but can hardly remember anything from Clason's book.

When I present in front of a room and need to use a flipchart, I either ask for a volunteer to scribe for me, or I make the joke "I trained to be a doctor, but only went to day one of the course, which was handwriting."

And when I speak on public stages, in front of hundreds, and in some cases thousands, I do it without notes, having realized that I think more quickly than I can read. By the time my first slide comes up, I have already listened to a recording of my own voice, hundreds of times, so the presentation is (almost) seamless.

I wonder how many tips like this would help others take off their self-imposed shackles and reach their potential?

If you're reading this and have suggestions to how my legacy can continue to build, please reach out. As almost a self-fulfilling prophecy, the process of writing *Infinite Legacy* has helped me begin to codify my own legacy project.

Whatever you decide your legacy will be, we are sure that it will be a result of many different influences that have caused you to take on a project that is meaningful to you today and will benefit future generations.

CHAPTER 24
INFINITE LEGACY AND THE 7 PRINCIPLES

In our previous book, *Infinite Giving: The 7 Principles of Givers Gain*, we had a chapter called The Rock Tumbler. It detailed the story of a young Steve Jobs and how he first learned the importance of teamwork, and all things working together with a little bit of grit and time to yield incredible results. We wrote that only when you combined Givers Gain with the 7 Principles and apply them equally in life, would you achieve Infinite Giving. The same is true if you want to achieve Infinite Legacy.

But giving and legacy are two very different things. You can maintain and control your giving activities, but, at some point, your legacy will be left in the hands of others.

So here we would recommend layering as many of the 7 Principles as possible, while you can. Leaving out just a single one will drastically reduce the chances of your legacy perpetuating on after you have gone and becoming infinite.

If you left out Principle 1, Be proud of the legacy you leave…

You will be working toward establishing something that, for whatever reason, is not in line with your own moral code. Chances are you will either give up all together, or others will see this personal conflict as it reflects their own code, and your legacy will never be secure and may be questioned or removed at a later date.

If you left out Principle 2, Give what you can afford when you can afford it…

You will be sacrificing your current time, energy, and resources, and neglecting the world around you NOW. You will find it more difficult to influence others to join you on your legacy journey as you will be running on empty and appearing desperate. Desperation is not a legacy anyone wants to be involved with.

If you left out Principle 3, Be guided by your passion…

Without passion you will not be able to weather the storm of early setbacks or have the energy to sustain your efforts. With passion comes belief, and with belief comes certainty; always follow your passion.

If you left out Principle 4, Connect with your community…

You will be ignoring you greatest allies, people like you who will have similar likes, beliefs, passions, and drives. By focusing locally, the core of each person's network will overlap and there will also be unique connections and skills that will help your legacy take flight.

If you left out Principle 5, Act with urgency…

You may never get the opportunity to leave your legacy to the world. Legacy is a today activity; don't wait until tomorrow.

If you left out Principle 6, Think like a stonemason…

You may focus only on the minutia of day-to-day tasks and lose sight of the overall goal. In the early days this can be disheartening, and, even as your legacy project grows, you will still need to focus on the spire of the cathedral. Even if you never personally see the spire completed, once it is finished it will inspire and bring hope to people for years to come.

If you left out Principle 7, Have an infinite mindset…

You may make decisions for short-term gain and not the longevity of your legacy. When we embrace an infinite mindset, there is a comfort knowing that not only will our legacy outlive us, but also it will continue to grow and take on a life of its own, for the benefit of all that encounter it.

Building an Infinite Legacy will require all of the above principles. They will act as your guide, and in some cases, your armor.

Many people make an impact and many more, in some small way, leave a legacy. Only when we combine all of the principles, do we have a chance of leaving an Infinite Legacy.

CHAPTER 25
THE DASH BETWEEN THE YEARS

There is an amazing poem that we highly recommend written by Linda Ellis called *"The Dash."* The opening lines of the poem say:

"I read of a man who stood to speak at a funeral of a friend. He referred to the dates on the tombstone from the beginning… to the end.

He noted that first came the date of birth and spoke of the following date with tears, but he said what mattered most of all was the dash between those years."

He noted that first came the date of birth and spoke of the following date with tears, but he said what mattered most of all was the dash between those years."

It goes on to say that the dash represents the time they spent on earth and how they lived their life. This is, in our opinion, the most powerful poem ever written about one's legacy and we urge you to purchase the entire poem, which is available online.

We have also mentioned another quote in this book: *"One always dies too soon or too late and yet their life is complete at that moment, with a line drawn neatly under it ready for the summing up"* by Jean Paul Sartre.

Both quotes are particularly relevant and incredibly powerful regarding the legacy we leave in life. When we think about and then embrace our legacy, we can extend that line or that dash far beyond the numbers on the memorial and to an infinite vanishing point.

We all have people who are in our story. They have changed our life in some important way. It might have been something small they did or many things over a long period of time. In either case, they have left a positive mark on our life. The only thing more important than *"Who's in our story?"* is *"Whose story are we in?"* Whose life have we changed in some positive way?

The only thing more important than "Who's in our story?" is "Whose story are we in?" Whose life have we changed in some positive way?

As individuals, what have we said, or what have we done, that has helped someone in some important way? Who have we positively impacted, so that we may be part of their story? That's a legacy anyone can leave. You don't have to be a millionaire to be in someone's story. You may not make a world of difference, but you can make a difference in the world and you do that one person at a time.

Hopefully, by now you have at the very least considered what your current legacy is. Maybe you have begun to think about what you would like it to be. Ultimately, we would love for you to begin your own legacy project, something that you will be proud to represent you when you are not able to represent yourself.

You may not make a world of difference, but you can make a difference in the world and you do that one person at a time.

Your legacy is your gift. Make it the very best gift you can bestow.

BNI

BNI, the world's largest business networking organization, was founded by Dr. Ivan Misner in 1985 as a way for businesspeople to generate referrals in a structured, professional environment. The organization, now the world's largest referral business network, has thousands of chapters with hundreds of thousands of members on every populated continent. Since its inception, BNI members have passed millions of referrals, generating billions of dollars in business for the participants.

The primary purpose of the organization is to pass qualified business referrals to its members. The philosophy of BNI may be summed up in two simple words: Givers Gain®. If you give business to people, you will get business from them. BNI allows only one person per profession to join a chapter. The program is designed to help businesspeople develop long-term relationships, thereby creating a basis for trust and, inevitably, referrals. The mission of BNI is to help members increase their business through a structured, positive, and professional word-of-mouth program that enables them to develop long-term, meaningful relationships with quality business professionals.

To visit a chapter near you, contact BNI visit its website at www.bni.com.

BIOGRAPHY
IVAN MISNER, PH.D.

Dr. Ivan Misner is the Founder & Chief Visionary Officer of BNI, the world's largest business networking organization. Founded in 1985, the organization now has over 11,100 chapters in over 75 countries throughout every populated continent of the world. Last year alone, BNI passed millions of referrals resulting in billions of dollars' worth of business for its members each year.

Dr. Misner's Ph.D. is from the University of Southern California. He is a *New York Times* Bestselling author who has written 30 books including his newest – *Infinite Legacy*. He is also a columnist for Entrepreneur.com and has been a university professor at several universities as well as a member of the Board of Trustees for the University of La Verne.

Called the *"Father of Modern Networking"* by both Forbes and CNN, Dr. Misner is considered to be one of the world's leading experts on business networking and has been a keynote speaker for major corporations and associations throughout the world. He has been featured in the *L.A. Times, Wall Street Journal,* and *New York Times,* as well as numerous TV and radio shows including *CNN,* the *BBC,* and *The Today Show* on *NBC.*

He has traveled to all seven continents of the world, including Antarctica. Among his many awards, he has been named "*Humanitarian of the Year*" by the Red Cross and has been the recipient of the *John C. Maxwell Leadership Award.* He is the Co-Founder of the BNI Charitable Foundation and is married to Jody Misner. ***Oh, and in his spare time!!!*** he is also an amateur magician and a black belt in karate.

BIOGRAPHY
GREG DAVIES

Greg knows he has the very best job in the world, in fact he feels slightly embarrassed about calling it a job.

Known as the Storyfella, he uses his passion for telling stories to help businesses and communities thrive, and people overcome limiting beliefs and avoidance behaviours.

After working in both large corporations and owning his own small business, he understands that working hard is sometimes unavoidable and necessary, but says "that's ok, as long as we understand *why* we are doing it, and we surround ourselves with those people who inspire us to be better, every single day."

A bestselling author, multi-award winning director of BNI, President of the Founder's Circle, corporate trainer, and international inspirational speaker, Greg still finds time to drum with the mighty **Goat Patrol** and is a not so secret Disney fan, citing the first as the ultimate stress relief, and the second as his, Franky's, and his two daughters' happy place.

BIOGRAPHY
JULIAN LEWIS

Julian believes in the power of collaboration for personal and business success. He envisions a world where everyone can achieve their success simultaneously. His mission is to empower people in business to create the success they desire through the power of collaboration and co-creation.

Julian is a seasoned portfolio entrepreneur. In 1999, he established his first business, an IT Support company, which he continues to own, and it has traded profitably every year. He is an esteemed BNI Executive Director based in the United Kingdom and a Founding Partner of the highly successful business coaching company Integrus Global.

Julian is the co-author of the Amazon Best-Seller *Infinite Giving— the 7 Principles of Givers Gain*, which he co-authored with Dr Ivan Misner, Ph.D., the founder of BNI, and "The Storyfella," Greg Davies.

Julian's heart beats for rugby union, a sport he played for 30 years. To unwind, he enjoys live rugby matches, cycling with friends, and celebrating life with positive people. He also shares his love for Arsenal (Soccer Club) with his two sons.

He is happily married to Linda, and they work together to create their perfect Life Blend. They have five grown-up children between them.

Made in the USA
Monee, IL
11 January 2025